GRAND CANYON TRIVIA

DON LAGO

RIVERBEND
PUBLISHING

Updated and revised in 2014.

Published by Riverbend Publishing, Helena, Montana.

Printed in the United States of America.

6 7 8 9 0 MG 20 19 18 17 16

Text design by Suzan Glosser
Cover design by Bob Smith

ISBN 10: 1-60639-004-X
ISBN 13: 978-1-60639-004-7

Riverbend Publishing
P.O. Box 5833
Helena, MT 59604
1-866-787-2363
www.riverbendpublishing.com

Contents

ACKNOWLEDGMENTS

A special thanks to Janet Spencer and Scott Thybony, and for the accuracy of this book, thanks to Kim Besom, Mike Quinn, Colleen Hyde, Mike Anderson, Larry Stevens, Tom Pittenger, Amy Horn, Ellen Brennan, Stew Fritts, Wayne Ranney, Richard Quartaroli, Brad Dimock, Tom Myers, Lon Ayers, Marker Marshall, Stewart Aitchison, Jim Heywood, Pat and Ron Brown, Betty Upchurch, Earle Spamer, Tom Martin, Matt Kaplinski, and Clio.

GEOGRAPHY

Q. How long is the Grand Canyon?
A) 35 miles (56 km)   B) 277 miles (445 km)   C) 1,450 miles (2,333 km)
A. B) 277 miles (445 km). You can drive along the South Rim for 35 miles, and there are overlooks where you can see at least 35 miles of the canyon, but 35 miles is only 12 percent of the Grand Canyon's 277. The canyon's length is measured by the miles of the Colorado River flowing through it.

Q. While the length of the Grand Canyon is measured by the Colorado River, the rim itself, which jigsaws in and out, is much longer. If you were to walk the length of the South Rim, how many miles would you walk?
A) 573 miles (921 km)   B) 973 miles (1,565 km)   C) 1,373 miles (2,209 km).
A. C) 1,373 miles (2,209 km). The North Rim is even longer: 1,384 miles (2,226 km).

Q. How deep is the Grand Canyon?
  A) One mile (1.6 km)   B) Two miles (3.2 km)   C) Five miles (8 km)
A.   A) One mile (1.6 km), or about 5,000 feet. But this depends somewhat on where you are measuring. The North Rim is higher than the South Rim, about 8,200 feet (2,500 m) in elevation compared with the South Rim's 7,000 feet (2,133 m). And each rim has variations. On the South Rim, El Tovar Hotel is 6,920 feet (2,109 m) in elevation, while Navajo Point is at 7,498 feet (2,285 m). On the North Rim, Grand Canyon Lodge is at 8,200 feet (2,500 m), while Point Imperial is at 8,803 feet (2,683 m). Also, the bottom of the canyon continues getting deeper as the Colorado River flows west. Below Point Imperial the river level is 2,800 feet (853 m) in elevation, while below El Tovar Hotel the river is 2,400 feet (731 m). It makes sense to average these differences and say the canyon is one mile deep.

Q. If you took the highest point in the eastern United States, Mt. Mitchell in North Carolina, and placed it inside the Grand Canyon, how much of it would stick out?
   A) None   B) 1/4th C) 1/2
A. B) 1/4th. Mt. Mitchell is 6,684 feet high (2037 m), so it doesn't quite fit into the Grand Canyon's 5,000-foot (1,524 m) depth. But one of the tallest mountains in New England, Mt. Katahdin, at 5,268 feet (1,605 m), would almost disappear. The highest points in 32 U.S. states would disappear inside the Grand Canyon.

Q. The highest elevation in Florida is 345 feet (105 m). How many Floridas could you stack up like pancakes inside the Grand Canyon?
   A) 5   B) 10   C) 15
A. C) 15 Floridas could be stacked up inside the Grand Canyon.

"The Yosemite? Dumped into this wilderness of gorges and mountains, it would take a guide a long time to find it."
—Charles Dudley Warner

In fact, since Yosemite Valley is seven miles (11 km) long, you could line up about 40 Yosemite Valleys along the Grand Canyon's 277-mile (445 km) length, and you could hide many more Yosemite Valleys in the Grand Canyon's side canyons.

Q. If you took Lake Superior, the deepest of the Great Lakes, and placed it inside the Grand Canyon, would it reach the rim?
A. Not even close. Lake Superior is 1,330 feet (405m) deep, so you'd have to stack up four Lake Superiors to overflow the Grand Canyon. Lake Baikal in Russia, the world's deepest lake at 5,315 feet (1,620 m), is the only lake as deep as the Grand Canyon.

Q. If Niagara Falls plunged into the Grand Canyon, how many times longer would it have to be to reach the bottom of the canyon?
   A) 10 times   B) 18 times   C) 28 times
A. C) 28 times longer.

The Grand Canyon is one of the seven natural wonders of the world.

Q. True or false: The highest waterfall inside the Grand Canyon is higher than Niagara Falls.
A. True. Mooney Falls (in a side canyon called Havasu) is 196 feet high (59 m), compared with Niagara's 182 feet. If you include non-sheer falls inside the Grand Canyon, then Cheyava Falls, which pours over a series of ledges, is 800 feet high (243 m).

Q. The tallest waterfall in the world is Angel Falls in Venezuela. If Angel Falls was falling into the Grand Canyon, would it touch the bottom?
A. Not even close. Angel Falls is 3,212 feet (979 m), only about 60 percent of the depth of the Grand Canyon.

> "It seems a gigantic statement for even nature to make."
> —John Muir

Q. The Great Pyramid of Giza was the tallest of the seven wonders of the ancient world. How many could you stack up inside the Grand Canyon?
    A) 5   B) 7   C) 11
A. C) 11. The Great Pyramid is 481 feet high (146 m).

> "A chasm...in which the pyramids, seen from the rim, would appear only like large tents."   —John Burroughs

Q. If you stacked up Empire State Buildings on top of one another, how many would it take to reach the rim of the Grand Canyon?
    A) 2   B) 4   C) 10
A. B) 4. The Empire State Building is 1,250 feet tall (381 m) from the base to the roof.

Q. The Olympic record for the high jump is 7.9 feet (2.4 m). How many times higher would a human have to jump to jump out of the Grand Canyon?
    A) 200   B) 650   C) 5,000
A. B) About 650 times.

Q. How far apart are the North Rim and the South Rim?
    A) 10 miles (16 km)   B) 21 miles (33 km)   C) 215 miles (345 km)
A. All of the above. For a raven, it's about ten miles, which is

---

The moon has two features called a Grand Canyon.

the average width of the canyon (the width varies from place to place, as the rims jag in and out). For a hiker, it's about 21 miles (33 km) on the North and South Kaibab Trail. For a driver, it's 215 miles (345 km).

Q. At its widest spot, how wide is the Grand Canyon?
   A) 10 miles (16 km)   B) 18 miles (29 km)   C) 25 miles (40 km)
A. B) 18 miles (29 km).

Q. How many Golden Gate Bridges would it take to reach across the Grand Canyon?
   A) 1   B) 5   C) 12
A. C) 12. The Golden Gate Bridge is 4,200 feet long (1280 m). The Grand Canyon is, on average, ten miles across, or more than 50,000 feet (15,240 m).

Q. The longest motorcycle ramp jump was 277 feet (84 m). How many times farther would a motorcyclist have to jump to cross the Grand Canyon?
   A) 100 times farther   B) 150 times C) 190 times
A. C) 190 times farther. (When Robbie Knievel did his Grand Canyon motorcycle jump, he actually only jumped a side canyon about 200 feet (60 m) wide).

"The Grand Canyon is something that all astronauts look for from space, and everyone is as excited as a child when they spot it for the first time."
   —astronaut Ken Bowersox

Q. Piffles are the Styrofoam nuggets used to cushion items for shipping. Earle Spamer of the Academy of Natural Sciences calculated how many semi-truck trailers full of piffles it would take to fill up the Grand Canyon. How many?
   A) 500 million   B) 750 million   C) 1 billion
A. B) To be exact: 756,685,947 trailers full of piffles.

Q. Why is the North Rim higher than the South Rim?
A. The plateau that encompasses the Grand Canyon slopes

The Grand Canyon was one of UNESCO's first "World Heritage Sites"...

toward the south. The plateau behind the North Rim is 9,000 feet (2,743 m) high; the North Rim is about 8,200 feet (2500 m) high; and the South Rim is about 7,000 feet (2133 m) high.

Q. Why is the North Rim farther from the Colorado River than the South Rim?
A. Since the plateau slopes toward the south, rain that falls on the plateau behind the North Rim flows toward the canyon, but rain that falls on the plateau behind the South Rim flows away from the canyon. Thus the north side of the canyon has more erosion, which has resulted in longer drainages to the river. The north side also has longer ridges and mesas, and more springs. On the North Rim there are only two overlooks from which you can see the river. On the South Rim you get a steeper look into the canyon, and you can often see the river.

Q. Where does the Grand Canyon end?
A. At Grand Wash Cliffs, 277 miles (445 km) downstream from where it begins at Lees Ferry, or about 190 miles (305 km) downstream from the visitor areas on the rims. The Grand Wash Cliffs mark a fault line where the canyon's cliffs drop abruptly and the Colorado River flows into open desert.

There's only one Grand Canyon on Earth. It took several rare ingredients to make the Grand Canyon.
1. Rock layers. The Grand Canyon reveals one mile and nearly two billion years of rocks. Nowhere else on Earth is the geological story so well displayed.
2. Uplift. The rocks had to be lifted a mile and a half into the air. Usually when so much rock is lifted so high, the rock layers fall apart. It's very unusual that a rock layer cake rises so high and remains intact.
3. A great river. It takes a lot of erosional power to carve a Grand Canyon.
4. A desert environment. If the Grand Canyon received more rain, it already would have eroded into just a wide valley.

Q. Why are there so many famous landscapes near the Grand Canyon, such as Zion, Bryce, Canyonlands, Arches, Monument

...a list that includes 166 natural areas, 12 of which are in the U.S.

Valley, Canyon de Chelly, the Painted Desert, and the Sedona red rocks?
A. They are all part of the Colorado Plateau, a geological province that covers 130,000 square miles (333,333 square km) in the Four Corners states Utah, Arizona, New Mexico, and Colorado. The Colorado Plateau is made of sedimentary rock that erodes into dramatic shapes and colors. The Grand Canyon lies on the western edge of the Colorado Plateau; it formed here because the Colorado River is draining off the Colorado Plateau into the low deserts to the west. Similarly, Zion Canyon and the red rocks of Sedona are notches on the edge of the Colorado Plateau.

Q. How hot does it get at the bottom of the Grand Canyon?
   A) 90 degrees F (32 C)   B) 106 F (41 C)   C) 120 F (49 C)
A. C) 120 degrees F (49 C). In the summer most days exceed 100 degrees (38 C). It can be 100 as early as April or as late as October. July highs average 106 (41 C). In a real heat wave, highs can hit 115 (46 C) for days at a time at Phantom Ranch, the guest lodge that holds the only official weather station along the Colorado River. But the Colorado River descends another 1,000 feet (304 m) below Phantom Ranch, and river guides sometimes report temperatures of 120 degrees F (49 C) or more.

Q. Why is it hotter at the bottom of the Grand Canyon than on the rim?
A. Heat is also a measure of air density, and air is thinner at higher elevations. With every 1,000 feet (304 m) of elevation gained, temperatures drop by about 5 degrees (2.7 C). Since the rim of the Grand Canyon is 5,000 feet (1,524 m) above the bottom, rim temperatures are typically 20 to 30 degrees cooler (11 to 16 C) than the bottom of the canyon. The same law of physics that makes it hotter at the bottom of the canyon also makes it harder to catch your breath in the thinner air on the rim.

Q. Elevation makes a big difference in how much precipitation falls. The North Rim gets 25 inches (63.5 cm) of precipitation per year, while the South Rim, which is one thousand feet (304

Mars has a canyon 3,000 miles long (4,827 km)...

m) lower, gets 15 inches (38 cm). Phantom Ranch is more than 4,000 feet (1219 m) below the South Rim. How much precipitation does Phantom Ranch get?

A) 12 inches (30 cm)   B) 9 inches (23 cm)   C) 4 inches (10 cm)

A. B) 9 inches. Much of the rain that falls from clouds above the ranch evaporates before it reaches the bottom of the canyon.

Q. What's the wettest month at the Grand Canyon?

A) April   B) August   C) December

A. B) August. Summers at the Grand Canyon bring a monsoon season with heavy afternoon rains. In August the South Rim receives 2.32 inches of rain (5.9 cm). April showers add up to only 0.87 inches (2.2 cm). December is the wettest winter month, with 1.69 inches (4.3 cm), mostly in the form of snow.

Q. What's the driest month at the Grand Canyon?

A) May   B) June   C) July

A. B) June. Though July and August have higher average temperatures than June, they also have monsoon rains. June sees only 0.39 inches (1 cm) of rain on the South Rim, while July sees 1.94 inches (4.9 cm). The second driest month is May, at 0.65 inches (1.6 cm).

Q. When does spring begin at the Grand Canyon?

A) March   B) April   C) May

A. All of the above. It starts at different times for different parts of the Grand Canyon. Just as it is springtime in Florida while it is still winter in Maine, spring starts in the Mohave Desert end of the Grand Canyon and moves up the river corridor. Likewise, spring moves vertically up the cliffs: wildflowers may flourish at Phantom Ranch while there's still lots of snow on the North Rim. On the South Rim, spring may not be going strong until May.

Q. In 1889 biologist C. Hart Merriam proposed that North America consists of seven life zones, geographical belts where temperature differences result in different ecosystems. Merriman conceived this idea while visiting the Grand Canyon

...ten times the length of Earth's Grand Canyon.

region. He noticed that altitudes could produce the same results as latitudes, that going from the North Rim to the Colorado River is like traveling from Canadian mountains to Mexican deserts. Of his seven life zones, how many are found at the Grand Canyon?

   A) 3   B) 5   C) 7

A. B) 5. The Grand Canyon lacks only the opposite extremes of the arctic and the subtropical life zones.

Q. How many species of plants live at the Grand Canyon?

   A) 500   B) 1,000   C) 1,800

A. B) About 1,800. This represents nearly half of the plant species in Arizona, which has the fourth highest number of plants in the U.S. (after California, Texas, and Florida). The Grand Canyon has nearly as many plant species as the Everglades.

Q. Other places have tried to claim some of the glory of the Grand Canyon by calling a landscape a Grand Canyon, such as the Grand Canyon of Missouri. How many states have a Grand Canyon?

   A) 3   B) 23   C) 43

A. C) 43. And 73 nations claim to have a Grand Canyon.

Q. Who coined the term "Grand Canyon"?

A. It was widely popularized by John Wesley Powell, who led the first Colorado River expedition in 1869. But the name was already in the air before Powell. It first appeared on a map in 1868.

Q. When did humans first discover the Grand Canyon?

A. The oldest human-made object found at the Grand Canyon is part of a Clovis point, used for hunting Ice Age animals like mammoths. It is about 12,000 years old.

Q. The first detailed topographical map of the Grand Canyon was made by:

   A) Satellites   B) Airplanes   C) Foot

A. C) Foot. In 1902 cartographer Francois Matthes arrived at the Grand Canyon and began years of carrying surveying equipment

---

Between 4 and 5 million people visit the Grand Canyon every year.

into the most rugged depths of the Grand Canyon. His map is still used today. Matthes also mapped Yosemite, Mt. Rainier, and the San Andreas Fault.

Q. Has anyone climbed the buttes and peaks inside the Grand Canyon?
A. Yes, hundreds of summits inside the canyon have been climbed. But the Grand Canyon isn't a climber's magnet like Yosemite because the canyon's sedimentary rock is weak and fragile compared to Yosemite's hard, secure granite.

Q. When did tourists start coming to the Grand Canyon?
A. In the 1880s, but in very small numbers. Only in 1901, when the Santa Fe Railway built tracks to the South Rim, did it become easy for tourists to reach the Grand Canyon. The Santa Fe Railway also built most of the tourist facilities along the South Rim. The Santa Fe Railway arrived at the canyon 18 years before the National Park Service did.

Q. Before the construction of the railroad to the Grand Canyon, most tourists arrived by stagecoach from Flagstaff. The route was a bumpy and dusty 73 miles (117 km), with three rest stations along the way. How many hours did this trip take?
    A) 4 hours   B) 8 hours   C) 12 hours
A. C) 12 hours, but it probably felt much longer!

America was the first nation to establish national parks. National parks are a very democratic idea the idea that natural wonders should belong to all citizens. If it weren't for national parks, places like the Grand Canyon, Yosemite, and Yellowstone could have been ruined by commercial development such as mining and logging, or they could have become the private property of the wealthy. Much of the world has copied the idea of America's national parks.

Q. America's first national park was Yellowstone in 1872. When did the Grand Canyon become a national park?
    A) 1873   B) 1895   C) 1919
A. C) 1919, nearly half a century after Yellowstone. While

About 60% of visitors are at the Grand Canyon for the first time.

Americans quickly recognized the value of the Grand Canyon and proposed making it into a national park, Arizona politicians vigorously opposed this, saying it would interfere with private mining, grazing, and logging. Today, Grand Canyon tourism pumps hundreds of millions of dollars into the Arizona economy, where 10 percent of jobs are tourism-related.

Q. Which president created Grand Canyon National Park?
   A) Benjamin Harrison   B) Teddy Roosevelt   C) Woodrow Wilson
A. All three played important roles. Woodrow Wilson signed the 1919 bill to establish Grand Canyon National Park. Benjamin Harrison first proposed a Grand Canyon National Park while still a senator in the 1880s. As president, Harrison made the Grand Canyon into a national forest preserve. In 1908 President Teddy Roosevelt promoted the Grand Canyon into a national monument. In 1975 President Gerald Ford signed a bill that greatly expanded the size of the park.

Q. What is the largest national park?
   A) Grand Canyon   B) Yellowstone   C) Wrangell-St. Elias
A. C) Wrangell-St. Elias in Alaska, at 8.3 million acres (3.3 million hectares). Six other Alaska national parks rank in the top ten. Yellowstone is 8th overall at 2.2 million acres (0.88 ha). The Grand Canyon is 11th at 1.2 million acres (0.48 ha), or 1,904 square miles (4,882 sq km). Of course, if you counted the surface area of all those cliffs, Grand Canyon National Park would be about 25 percent larger!

Q. What portion of the state of Arizona is occupied by Grand Canyon National Park?
   A) Less than 2 percent   B) 10 percent   C) 25 percent
A. A) Less than 2 percent. Grand Canyon National Park is larger than only one state, Rhode Island. Of course, the significance of national parks isn't measured by the size of their boundaries.

Q. While the river and the shore inside the Grand Canyon belong to the National Park Service, much of the land on the south side of the canyon belongs to someone else. Who is this?

Up to 40 percent of Grand Canyon visitors are from outside the U.S. ...

A. Three Native American tribes, the Navajos, the Hualapais, and the Havasupais. Together the tribes own a majority of the distance along the south side of the Grand Canyon.

Q. Since the Colorado River runs through the Grand Canyon, some people mistakenly suppose that the Grand Canyon lies in the state of Colorado. In 1999 the U. S. Postal Service printed up a stamp captioned "Grand Canyon, Colorado." As soon as someone noticed the mistake, all the stamps were destroyed. How many incorrect stamps were printed?

    A) 10,000   B) 1 million   C) 100 million

A. C) 100 million. Then the Post Office tried again and printed 100 million stamps that said "Grand Canyon, Arizona." But only after the stamps were in circulation did someone notice that the photo of the Grand Canyon was backwards.

> In the 1960s the American Automobile Association produced an Arizona highway map that showed the hiking trails to Phantom Ranch as highways, leaving motorists imagining they could drive through the Grand Canyon.

Q. Where is Lees Ferry?

    A) On the rim of the Grand Canyon   B) At the bottom   C) Both

A. C) Both! Lees Ferry, located just off Highway 89A, is the official beginning of the Grand Canyon. You can drive right up to the Colorado River. Standing beside it, you are standing on both the rim and the bottom of the canyon. Looking downstream, you see the river dropping and the cliffs rising. Lees Ferry is where Grand Canyon river trips begin.

Q. Besides at Lees Ferry, is there any road that lets you drive to the bottom of the Grand Canyon?

A. Only one, a bad, rocky, 22-mile (35 km) road that goes down a creek bed. After a thunderstorm, the road can be impassible. This road heads down from Peach Springs, Arizona, a Hualapai Indian town, and reaches the river 225 miles (362 km) downstream from Lees Ferry. Many river trips end here.

Q. Many of the rock formations inside the Grand Canyon have mythological names. There's an Egyptian section, including Isis

...a higher percentage than for most national parks.

Temple and the Tower of Ra. There's a Greek and Roman section, including Apollo Temple and Venus Temple. There's a Hindu section, a Norse section, even a King Arthur section. Who decided to give mythological names to the Grand Canyon?

A. A geologist named Clarence Dutton. Dutton was well read in literature and mythology. When he saw the Grand Canyon in the 1870s he felt that it was so magnificent that only the names of gods could do justice to it. The canyon peaks reminded Dutton of human architecture, so he called many of them temples. Subsequent surveyors continued Dutton's mythological tradition. Dutton himself is commemorated by Dutton Point.

> "It is all Beethoven's nine symphonies in stone and magic light. Even to remember that it is still there lifts the heart."
>   —J. B. Priestly

Q. What is the common theme in the names of these canyon formations: Darwin Plateau, Wallace Butte, Huxley Terrace, and Evolution Amphitheater?

A. The first three were named for scientists who advanced the theory of biological evolution: Charles Darwin, Alfred Russel Wallace, and Thomas Huxley.

Q. There's a Bright Angel Creek, a Bright Angel Point, a Bright Angel Trail, a Bright Angel Lodge, a Bright Angel Canyon, and the Bright Angel Shale. Where did this name come from?

A. It was given by John Wesley Powell, leader of the first Colorado River expedition in 1869. Powell and his men were tired, hungry, and discouraged, but camping beside a clear, lively stream lifted their spirits. Powell took the name from a Methodist hymn. Author Marguerite Henry used the name Brighty for the burro hero of her classic novel, *Brighty of the Grand Canyon*.

Q. In addition to Bright Angel, are there any other canyon formations named for Judeo-Christian themes?

A. There's Angels Gate, Angels Window, Trinity Creek, Holy Grail Temple, Christmas Tree Cave, The Transept, Hades Knoll, The Tabernacle, Solomon Temple, and Sheba Temple.

Horseshoe Mesa (below Grandview Point) got its name...

The Grand Canyon contains a spring called Thunder River, which gushes out of a cliff. After only a half mile Thunder River flows into Tapeats Creek, making it one of the shortest rivers in the world and almost the only river to flow into a creek.

Q. A natural stone bridge inside the Grand Canyon is named The Bridge of Sighs. What does this name mean?
A. The Kolb brothers (early Grand Canyon photographers) named it for a bridge in Venice, Italy, that once led condemned prisoners to the dungeon. The Kolbs thought that the gulch around the stone bridge was gloomy and prison-like.

One day a nature-loving couple came to the Grand Canyon. After many hours they left, but a few minutes later they came back to the entry station and explained that they had become so absorbed in watching wildlife in the forest that they "forgot to go look at the canyon." This true story makes an important point. The Grand Canyon may be an awesome sight, but there is much more to it than the view. There are many levels on which you can experience the Grand Canyon. With a little effort, you can see the Grand Canyon with the eyes of a geologist, an archaeologist, a Native American, a historian, a pioneer, a wildlife biologist, a botanist, an artist, a hiker, or a river rafter, and you can see whole new worlds of wonders.

...because it's shaped like a horseshoe.

Nautiloid Canyon (a Grand Canyon side canyon) was named for its fossilized sea creatures.

Mooney Falls was named for prospector Daniel Mooney who in 1880 fell over the falls to his death.

Every year the park awards 25,000 Junior Ranger badges.

Arizona doesn't go on Daylight Savings Time: in summer, it already has enough sunlight!

GEOLOGY

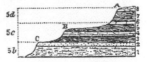

Q. Why did the Apollo astronauts hike into the Grand Canyon when they were training to go to the moon?
A. The astronauts needed to understand rocks, and the Grand Canyon offers the most dramatic geological textbook on Earth.

Q. What cut the Grand Canyon?
   A) The Colorado River   B) An earthquake   C) Glaciers
A. The Colorado River, plus erosion caused by precipitation.

Q. True or false: Because the Grand Canyon is much wider than the Colorado River, the river must have been much wider long ago.
A. False. The river has always been about the size it is today. The river has cut the depth of the canyon, but not its width. The width was cut by erosion from rain and snow falling into the sides of the canyon. Flash floods carry rock debris to the river, and the river carries away the debris like a conveyor belt.

Q. Exactly how did the Colorado River carve the Grand Canyon?
A. Good question! Though geologists have studied the Grand Canyon for 150 years, they are still debating exactly how it was carved. The biggest puzzle is why the Colorado River charges straight into a huge uplift, the Kaibab Plateau. Rivers are supposed to flow away from higher ground. John Wesley Powell proposed that the Colorado River had established its course first, and then the land rose around it. Today the answer seems more complicated: several ancestral rivers combined to form the Colorado River as the land rose in some places, dropped in other places, and eroded massively in many places. As the land rose, the flow of part of the river may have even reversed direction. The exact details are still a puzzle.

Q. Is the Grand Canyon getting deeper?
A. Yes, but not as fast as it once did. The layer of black rock at the bottom of the Grand Canyon, called schist, is much harder

than the layers of sedimentary rock above it, so as soon as the Colorado River reached the schist, the carving slowed down.

Q. Where did the rock and dirt that eroded out of the Grand Canyon end up?
A) The Rocky Mountains   B) The Pacific Ocean   C) In your hamburger
A. C) In your hamburger! Dirt from the Grand Canyon went down the Colorado River. The river drains into the Gulf of California, but the gulf's location has changed over millions of years. At one time the Gulf of California reached into what is now the Imperial Valley in California. The Colorado River built a large delta there, and that rich soil now supports one of the best agricultural areas in America. The lettuce in your hamburger may be made out of soil that eroded from the Grand Canyon five million years ago.

Q. How much rock was eroded away to form the Grand Canyon?
A) 10 cubic miles   B) 100 cubic miles   C) 1,000 cubic miles
A. C) About 1,000 cubic miles. This is enough rock and dirt to fill up about four million Houston Astrodomes!

> "Erosion, erosion—one sees in the West as never before that the world is shaped by erosion...In the East, the earth's wounds are virtually all healed, but in the West they are yet raw and gaping, if not bleeding."
> —John Burroughs

> John Hance was a 1880s prospector who became the Grand Canyon's first tourist guide. He also became a legendary teller of tall tales. Here's one of them:
> When John Hance first arrived in Arizona, there was no Grand Canyon, only a flat plain. Since Hance was a poor man, there was a hole in his pants pocket, out of which fell a nickel. Hance couldn't afford to lose a nickel, so he reached down to pick it up, but it slipped into a crack in the ground. He got out his shovel and dug for the nickel, but it slipped deeper and deeper. Refusing to give up, Hance continued digging until he looked up and found that he had dug the Grand Canyon.

Sedimentary rocks make up only 5 percent of Earth's crust...

Q. In reality, how long would it have taken John Hance to dig the Grand Canyon if he had dug out one bucket of dirt (let's define one bucket as one cubic foot of dirt) every minute for 24 hours a day for 365 days a year?
  A) 10,000 years   B) 1 million years   C) 280 million years
A. C) 280 million years. That's about 50 times longer than it took the Colorado River to carve the canyon.

Q. How much erosion of the Grand Canyon was done by wind?
A. Very little. Water is the big mover. Water acts quietly, seeping into cracks in rocks and then freezing and breaking rocks apart; and water acts violently, in flash floods that roll car-sized boulders toward the river. The Colorado River gains much of its erosive power from its silt, which acts like liquid sandpaper.

> The power of flash floods was shown by a flood that came down Crystal Creek in December, 1966. A combination of heavy rain and snowmelt gave the creek a bigger flow than the river itself. The flood rolled huge boulders into the river, building a dam that greatly constricted the river and created huge, irregular waves. Crystal Rapid had been a mild rapid, but today it's one of the most feared rapids in America. The same storm that created Crystal Rapid also brought floodwaters down Bright Angel Creek, wiping out footbridges and buildings at Phantom Ranch.

Q. Does the Grand Canyon have earthquakes?
A. Not big ones. The Grand Canyon is part of the Colorado Plateau, an unusually thick and stable part of Earth's crust. But the uplifting of the Colorado Plateau left lots of fault lines running north and south across the Grand Canyon. These faults broke up the rocks, making it easier for water to flow down fault lines. Many of the large side canyons in the Grand Canyon follow fault lines.
Most of the hiking trails take advantage of where faults have turned impassible cliffs into slopes of boulders.

...but 75 percent of the rocks exposed on its surface.

Q. True or false: The San Andreas Fault, which causes big earthquakes in California, helped create the Grand Canyon.
A. True, but in an indirect way. About 5 to 6 million years ago the San Andreas Fault opened up the Gulf of California. Until then, the Baja Peninsula was connected with the Mexican mainland. Until that time, it seems that the Colorado River didn't reach the sea, but drained into the high desert. The opening of the Gulf of California connected the Colorado River to sea level, which gave the river a much greater gradient and erosive power than it had before. Most of the Grand Canyon was carved rapidly about 5 to 6 million years ago.

Q. The Grand Canyon was carved about 5 to 6 million years ago, but how old is the rock exposed by the canyon?
  A) 10 million years   B) 500 million years   C) 1.75 billion years
A. C) The schist, the black rock at the bottom of the canyon, is 1.75 billon years old, or 340 times older than the canyon that exposed it. But in one spot, a side canyon called Elves Chasm, the rocks are nearly 100 million years older, or 1.84 billion years old.

Q. How can we tell the age of rocks?
A. Volcanic rocks contain radioactive isotopes that decay at a predictable rate. This allows us to date not only volcanic rocks, but the rock layers below and above volcanic rocks. We are relying on the same laws of radioactivity that we trust when we build atomic bombs and atomic reactors, so let's hope those laws are trustworthy!

Q. The rock at the bottom of the Grand Canyon is 1.75 billion years old. What percent of Earth's history does this age represent?
  A) 10 percent   B) 25 percent   C) 40 percent
A. C) About 40 percent of Earth's 4.6 billion year history.

Q. What percent of the universe's history is contained in Grand Canyon rocks?
  A) 5 percent   B) 13 percent   C) 50 percent
A. B) 13 percent. Astronomers now estimate that the universe is 13.7 billion years old, so Grand Canyon rocks represent about one-eighth of the age of the universe.

When the Kaibab Formation was deposited, North America lay...

"This incredible pageantry of sunlight and chasm...is our nearest approach to fourth-dimensional scenery...you feel that some elements of Time have been conjured into the immensities of Space. Perhaps it is not size nor the huge witchery of changing shapes and shades that fills us with awe, but the obscure feeling that here we have an instantaneous vision of innumerable eons."
—J. B. Priestly

Q. There are three basic types of rocks. Igneous rock is made of magma that arises from inside the earth and, if it reaches the surface, forms volcanoes and flows as lava. Sedimentary rock is made of sediments, tiny particles that collect at the bottom of an ocean, a lake, or even a desert, and eventually turn into rock. Metamorphic rock is either igneous or sedimentary rock that has been subjected to heat and pressure and turned into new forms of rock. Which type of rock makes up most of the Grand Canyon?

A) Igneous   B) Sedimentary   C) Metamorphic
A. B) Sedimentary rocks make up all but the bottom layer of the canyon, which is metamorphic rock.

Q. There are three types of sedimentary rocks: sandstone, limestone, and shale. What kinds of sediments make up these rocks?
A. The name sandstone gives you a pretty good clue: sand! Limestone is made out of the shells and skeletons of sea creatures. Shale is made of mud and silt.

Q. Why does the canyon have layers of different colors?
A. The layers are made of different kinds of rocks. Limestone is usually white or grey, and sandstone is red. The black layer at the bottom is schist. The Tonto platform (the terrace about three-fourths of the way down in the canyon) is greenish because it is shale. But sometimes limestone surfaces are turned red by iron leeching out of the rock layers above. This is why the tall cliffs about halfway down in the canyon are called the Redwall Limestone. When slabs fall off the Redwall Limestone, the newly exposed rock is white or gray.

...south of the equator and was part of the super continent Pangaea.

Q. Why are there distinct layers of sandstone, limestone, and shale in the canyon? What conditions caused different rocks to form?
A. The rock layers reveal how far out at sea that spot was when sediment was collecting there. When sediments are washing down a river and into the sea, the heaviest sediments settle out first. The heaviest sediment is sand, so sand settles out first, and sandstone indicates the area was close to shore. Because silt particles are lighter than sand, they can float farther out to sea. When they settle to the bottom, they form shale. Far out at sea there are no river sediments left in the water, so the only sediments are the shells and skeletons of dead sea creatures. They form limestone. Where the canyon contains a layer of limestone atop a layer of shale atop a layer of sandstone, this means that this spot was getting deeper under water over time.

Most of the rock layers in the Grand Canyon were formed when the Grand Canyon region lay beneath a shallow sea just off the west coast of the North American continent. The theory of plate tectonics says that continents can move, grow in size, collide, and rise and fall in elevation. The Grand Canyon offers a rich illustration of plate tectonics theory. The seabed and sea level were rising and falling as canyon rock layers were forming, and then this rock was raised a mile and a half above sea level.

Q. As river rafters head west on the Colorado River, they see some rock layers getting thicker and others getting thinner. Why is this?
A. In a way, they are traveling from the shallow, near-shore part of the ancient sea to deeper parts of the sea. As rafters head west, the rock layers that formed closest to the shore of the ancient sea become thinner, while the rock layers that formed farther at sea, such as the Redwall Limestone, become thicker.

Q. Some canyon rock layers form cliffs and some form slopes. This is because some layers of rock are harder and some are softer. Are the cliffs made of harder or softer rock?
A. Harder rock. The hardest rock forms the tallest cliffs, while the softest rock, the Bright Angel Shale, has left the largest slope, the Tonto platform.

The South Rim recedes 2.5 inches per century...

For hikers, geology isn't an abstraction. Hikers know when they go from one rock layer into another. The color of the trail changes, and so does its steepness. The steepest cliffs are formed by the hardest rocks. Hiking through the Redwall Limestone always involves 500 feet (152 m) of steep switchbacks.

Q. For river rafters too, geology is no abstraction. Erosion forms sharp edges on Muav Limestone. When the Muav Limestone is at river level, what threat does it pose to rafts?
A. Rafters use ropes to tie their rafts to shore at night. If a rope rubs against a Muav ledge all night, the sharp edge of rock might cut the rope and the raft could float away.

Q. How is hiking in the Grand Canyon like a science fiction movie?
A. Because the Grand Canyon is like a time machine. As you hike into it, you are, geologically speaking, traveling back in time.

Q. How far do you have to hike to place your hands on all the rock layers inside the Grand Canyon?
    A) 5 miles (8 km)   B) 10 miles (16 km)   C) 100 feet (30 m)
A. C) 100 feet (30 m). That's the distance from the front door of the Bright Angel Lodge to the History Room, where architect Mary Colter built a fireplace using rocks from all the rock layers inside the Grand Canyon. A mule wrangler helped gather the rocks and carry them up on mules.

There are places inside the Grand Canyon where a human hand can span more than a billion years of time. That's in the places where the rock record contains a gap of about 1.2 billion years because the missing rock was eroded away. John Wesley Powell called this gap the Great Unconformity. You can lay your palm on rock 1.7 billion years old and your fingers on rock 550 million years old. This gap is more typical of Earth's geological history than are the layers that remain: Earth's rocks are eroding away all the time. The Grand Canyon is exceptional in how much of Earth's history it preserves and makes visible. There are a few

...the North Rim recedes twice as fast.

sections of the canyon where most of these intermediary rock layers weren't eroded away; they are called the Grand Canyon Supergroup and date from 1.2 billion to 740 million years old.

"The rhythm of the rocks beats very slowly...The minute hand of its clock moves by the millions of years. But it moves. And its second hand moves by the ceaseless erod-ing drip of a seep spring, by the stinging flight of sand particles on a gray and windy evening, by the particle-on-particle accretion of white travertine in warm blue-green waters..."
                                                                —Colin Fletcher

Q. What kind of rock makes up the canyon rim?
A. The Kaibab Formation, which is mostly limestone. It's about 300 feet (91 m) thick and forms cliffs. It's a very tough rock, and doesn't erode easily.

Q. The Kaibab Formation is 270 million years old. Were there once younger rocks above this, and if so, what happened to them?
A. There used to be thousands of feet of rock layers above the Kaibab Formation, but they eroded away, at least near the Grand Canyon. But these rock layers still exist in nearby areas, such as southern Utah. The top layer of the Grand Canyon is the bottom layer of Zion National Park. Many of the rock layers above the Kaibab Formation were relatively soft rocks that eroded rapidly. But when erosion hit the Kaibab Formation, which is a very tough rock, it slowed way down. If it wasn't for the Kaibab Formation, erosion would have continued eating into lower rock layers, and the Grand Canyon wouldn't be the way it looks today.

Q. Why is the Kaibab Formation such a tough rock?
A. Because it's full of fossils. The Kaibab Formation is a lime-stone formed in an ocean full of life, such as sponges. When those creatures died, their bodies were replaced by silica par-ticles, forming hard nodules of chert. Sponges are the softest of life forms, but they turned into the hardest of rocks. These ancient life forms turned into the rock layer that resisted ero-sion and helped make the Grand Canyon the way it is today.

The words "erode" and "rodent" have the same Latin root: "rod", to gnaw.

Q. Can you see fossils in Grand Canyon rocks?
A. Yes, mainly in the limestone layers. If you hike into the canyon you can see the fossils changing form as the rocks become older. But you don't have to hike into the canyon to see fossils. Many visitors get so busy looking into the big geology of the canyon that they never notice the little geology at their feet. The Kaibab Formation is full of fossils such as corals, mollusks, crinoids, sponges, and brachiopods. Sometimes they are merely nodules of colored minerals, but sometimes they have the detailed shapes of life forms. A good place to see fossils on the surface is just west of the Hermit Road bus interchange (near the Bright Angel Lodge) as you follow the Rim Trail up the slope.

Q. How old are the oldest fossils in the Grand Canyon?
   A) 270 million years   B) 550 million years   C) 1.2 billion years
A. C) 1.2 billon years old. These fossils are stromatolites, formed by mats of blue-green algae that grew in a shallow coastal sea. Today in Australia you can find living stromatolites that look just like Grand Canyon fossil stromatolites.

Q. True or False: The Grand Canyon is full of dinosaur bones.
A. False. The Grand Canyon's rocks are older than the dinosaurs. Dinosaurs first appeared about 220 million years ago, but the youngest Grand Canyon rocks are 270 million years old.

Q. Ferns are the oldest vascular plant found in the world's fossil records, dating back about 400 million years. Fern fossils are found in the Grand Canyon. Do ferns live in the Grand Canyon today?
A. Yes, about 20 species. There's even a side canyon and a rapid called Fern Glen.

> Until 570 million years ago, life on Earth remained simple, single-celled organisms. Then in the "Cambrian explosion" life burst into a greater complexity of forms. By chance, the sedimentary rock record in the Grand Canyon starts at the time of the Cambrian explosion, so the canyon offers a rich history of evolution.

The Hermit Shale has imprints of raindrops and shore ripples.

Q. True or False: By looking at Grand Canyon rocks can you tell which way the wind was blowing 275 million years ago.
A. True. The Coconino Sandstone, which is the white "bathtub ring" three layers down from the rim, is the only layer formed in a desert environment. It consists of sand dunes piled up by ancient winds. The original slopes of the dunes are still visible, and they tell us which way the wind was blowing 275 million years ago.

Q. The Coconino Sandstone contains lizard-like tracks that often stop abruptly. What happened to the lizards?
   A) Died of heat   B) Grabbed by birds   C) Nothing
A. C) Nothing. Since lizards are cold-blooded they have to sun themselves, so they climb sand dunes early in the morning, when the sand is wet with dew and holds the imprint of lizard feet. By the time the lizards warm up and leave, the dew is gone so their footprints no longer hold together, and as lizards scurry down a sand dune, their tail erases their tracks.

Q. Are there any other fossil tracks in the Grand Canyon?
A. Yes. The Bright Angel Shale is full of trilobite tracks. The Hermit Shale has amphibian tracks.

Q. The bottom layer of the Grand Canyon is a black rock called schist. The schist started out as sedimentary rock, but tremen- dous pressures changed it into a new form of rock, so we call it a metamorphic rock. How much older is the schist than the youngest, top layer of the canyon?
   A) Twice as old   B) 3 times as old   C) 7 times as old
A. C) About 7 times as old. The schist is 1.75 billion years old, while the top layer, the Kaibab Formation, is 270 million years old.

Q. The Yavapai Observation Station on the South Rim once had a piece of schist and a steel file for visitors to use on the schist to see how hard the schist was. Why did the National Park Service decide to remove this exhibit?
A. The files were always wearing down and breaking. When visitors found that they couldn't even scratch the schist, they got frustrated and started stabbing it with the sharp handle of the file.

Trilobites, whose fossil tracks are found in the Bright Angel Shale...

Q. The black schist has veins of pinkish rock running through it. What is this?

    A) Lava   B) Granite   C) Marble

A. B) Granite. Granite is formed when magma tries to reach the surface. If magma reaches the surface it forms volcanoes and flows as lava. If it fails to reach the surface it cools underground and forms a very hard rock—granite.

Q. One of the most dramatic things about rafting through the Grand Canyon is that you see each rock layer emerging from the ground. Visitors on the rim can get a sense of this too. From the easternmost overlooks, Desert View on the South Rim and Point Imperial on the North Rim, you can't see the bottom rock layer—the black schist marbled with granite. From Grand Canyon Village on the South Rim and Grand Canyon Lodge on the North Rim, you can see it. Where in the canyon's 277-mile length does the schist emerge?

    A) Mile 50   B) Mile 77   C) Mile 125

A. B) Mile 77. This is at Hance Rapid, below Moran Point on the South Rim and Cape Royal on the North Rim.

A *mnemonic* is a device, such as a formula or rhyme, that helps us remember information. Here is a good mnemonic sentence for recalling the sequence of the Grand Canyon's rock layers from rim to canyon floor:

"Know The Canyon's History; Study Rocks Made By Time Very Slowly."

The first letter of each word in the sentence reminds us of these rock layers:

      Kaibab Formation
      Toroweap Formation
      Coconino Sandstone
      Hermit Formation
      Supai Group
      Redwall Limestone
      Muav Limestone
      Bright Angel Shale
      Tapeats Sandstone
      Vishnu Schist

...are related to today's horseshoe crabs.

Q. There are lots of cavities in the canyon cliffs. What are these?
  A) Mines   B) Caves   C) Landslides
A. B) Caves. While there are some old mines visible from the rim, they appear as mere specks and you have to know exactly where to look. The cavities you see everywhere are natural caves, mainly in the Redwall Limestone, produced by water seeping through the limestone and by external weathering. The Redwall Limestone is the same rock layer that forms Mammoth Cave in Kentucky. Grand Canyon National Park has more caves than any other national park.

Q. True or false: Volcanoes on the rim of the western Grand Canyon once built a lava dam in the Colorado River three times as high as Hoover Dam.
A. True. Nearly a million years ago the volcanoes in the Toroweap Valley poured out enough lava to dam the Colorado River. This happened several times. One dam was about 2,000 feet high (609 m), about three times the 730-foot (222 m) height of Hoover Dam, may have the tallest concrete dam in the United States. The lava dams may have turned the Colorado River into a lake hundreds of miles long. Eventually, rising water spilled over the lava dams and quickly tore them apart. Today the most famous rapid in the Grand Canyon, Lava Falls, is formed of remnants of these lava flows.

Q. Havasu Canyon is a side canyon famous for its pools of blue-green water. What forms these pools?
A. Travertine, a dissolved limestone that gives the water its blue-green color and solidifies into a hard deposit that forms dikes or dams in the creek, which creates the pools.

Q. Early in the 20th century it became popular for tourists to have their hats sent down into Havasu Canyon and hung on trees near the waterfalls there. Then the hats were sent back to the tourists. What was the purpose of hanging hats beside the Havasu waterfalls?
A. The mist rising from the waterfalls was full of travertine, and it coated the hats and stiffened them, just like bronzing a baby shoe. Travertine hats were a genuine souvenir of the Grand Canyon.

The Grand Canyon has more than 1,000 springs and seeps...

Q. Around 1950 a natural rock arch inside the Grand Canyon was discovered by a future U.S. presidential candidate. Who was he?
   A) John F. Kennedy   B) Barry Goldwater   C) Al Gore
A. B) Barry Goldwater. Senator Goldwater, a private pilot, was flying his airplane over the canyon when he spotted the arch. He named it Kolb Bridge for the Kolb brothers, famous Grand Canyon photographers. Actually, the arch was first discovered in 1871 but forgotten. In 1964 Goldwater was the Republican candidate for president.

Q. Has any gold been found inside the Grand Canyon?
A. Almost none. The canyon's sedimentary rocks aren't typical of where gold deposits occur. Early prospectors found tiny amounts of gold dust in river sandbars, washed down from above the canyon, but it wasn't enough to pay for mining it.

Q. Are there valuable minerals in the Grand Canyon?
A. Early prospectors found incredible deposits of asbestos and copper, some of the purest ores in the world. The Chicago World's Fair of 1893 displayed a 700-pound (320 kg) copper nugget, 70-percent pure, that came from the mines on Horseshoe Mesa. Still, by the time ores were hauled out of the canyon by mule, taken by horse and wagon to a distant railroad, and then shipped hundreds of miles to a smelter, the value of the copper didn't make the mining profitable enough to be worth all the trouble. In the 1950s geologists took a new look at an abandoned copper mine and found one of the richest uranium deposits in America. Uranium mining continued on the South Rim until 1969.

Q. True or false: Asbestos from the Grand Canyon was used to make theater curtains for the most famous theaters in London and Paris.
A. True. In the age before electricity, theaters were lit by lanterns, making fires a serious danger. Asbestos, a fireproofing material, was sewn inside theater curtains to reduce the danger of their catching fire. The asbestos from John Hance's mine was of such high quality that it was exported to Europe.

...10 percent of the canyon's plant species depend on them.

Q. Who was the first geologist to see the Grand Canyon?
A. John Strong Newberry in 1858. Newberry recognized that the canyon was the world's "most splendid exposure of stratified rocks." He recognized and named many of the rock layers.

Q. Newberry only saw the western end of the canyon. Who was the first geologist is to see the entire canyon?
A. John Wesley Powell.

Q. From what college did Powell get his geology degree?
   A) Harvard   B) Duke   C) None
A. C) None. Like many naturalists in the 19th century, Powell was largely self-taught. Many of Powell's observations and theories have stood up well.

Q. Why is it appropriate that a Grand Canyon butte is named "Lyell Butte"?
A. Charles Lyell was one of the founders of geology. His 1830 book, *Principles of Geology,* advanced the concept that given enough time, small but steady processes like rainfall and erosion could add up to the largest changes. The Grand Canyon is almost a rock version of Lyell's book and proof of his ideas.

To make the geological eras of the Grand Canyon easier to grasp, imagine the canyon's nearly 2 billion years as a 24-hour day, starting at midnight. It will be after dinner before the canyon rocks are finished being formed. It will be a few minutes before midnight when the Colorado River cuts into and exposes those rocks. It will be one-fifth of a second before midnight when humans start building cities and recording their history.

The Vishnu Schist was named for a Hindu god.

The Colorado Plateau and the Rocky Mountains were uplifted at the same time.

The Colorado River has no waterfalls, but lots of streams in side canyons do.

Grand Canyon side streams form many narrow, sinuous, slot canyons.

THE RIM

Q. The first white explorers to stand on the rim of the Grand Canyon were fooled by the canyon's scale. They thought that the Colorado River was just a little creek 6 feet (2 m) wide. In reality, how wide is the river?

A) 25 feet (8 m)   B) 100 feet (30 m)   C) 300 feet (91 m)

A. C) 300 feet (91 m) on average. The narrowest point is 76 feet (23 m).

Q. When you first look into the Grand Canyon, it can be tricky to grasp its scale. But there are a few features that can help, such as the trees at Phantom Ranch and Indian Garden. How tall are these trees?

A) 50 feet (15 m)   B) 75 feet (22 m)   C) 100 feet (30 m)

A. C) As tall as 100 feet (30 m). If you can see the black bridge across the Colorado River to Phantom Ranch, this is 440 feet (134 m) long. Specks of color in the river beside the bridge are rafts 16 to 18 feet (5 m) long.

Q. From the Grand Canyon's rims, how far can you see on the horizon?

A) 20 miles (32 km)   B) 60 miles (96 km)   C) 90 miles (144 km)

A. C) 90 miles (144 km). From some South Rim overlooks, such as Grandview and Desert View, you can see Navajo Mountain in Utah 90 miles away. From overlooks farther west, such as Hopi Point, you can see Mt. Trumbull and Mt. Logan 60 miles to the northwest, and plateaus well beyond them. From the North Rim, you can see the San Francisco volcanic range (between Flagstaff and Williams) some 60-70 miles away.

> "Nearly everybody, on taking a first look at the Grand Canyon, comes right out and admits its wonders are absolutely indescribable—and then proceeds to write anywhere from two thousand to fifty thousand words, giving full details."
> —Irwin S. Cobb

Q. What's the meaning of the overlook names on the South Rim?
A. Most were named for Southwestern Native American tribes: Hopi, Navajo, Mohave, Pima, Maricopa, Yavapai, Lipan, and Yaki. Most of these tribes never actually lived at the Grand Canyon. Four overlooks were named for Americans important in Grand Canyon history: Powell Point for river explorer John Wesley Powell; Moran Point for artist Thomas Moran; Mather Point for Stephen Mather the first director of the National Park Service; and Hermits Rest for prospector Louis Boucher. Three overlooks Grandview, Desert View, and Trailview tell you what you'll see.

Q. Stephen Mather had another career before he became the first director of the National Park Service. In his previous career he created a famous advertising symbol. What was it?
A) The Borax Soap 20-mule team   B) The RCA dog listening to the phonograph   C) The Budweiser Clydesdales
A. A) The Borax Soap 20-mule team. Mather worked for the Borax Company in Death Valley, and he fell in love with southwestern landscapes. As director of the National Park Service, Mather set standards that have made America's national park system the envy of the world.

Q. An overlook on the North Rim was named for a U. S. president. Which president?
A) Thomas Jefferson   B) Teddy Roosevelt   C) Dwight Eisenhower
A. B) Roosevelt Point was named for Teddy Roosevelt, a great conservationist. Roosevelt loved the Grand Canyon and visited it several times, and in 1908 he made the Grand Canyon into a national monument.

"Leave it as it is...The ages have been at work on it, and man can only mar it. What you can do is to keep it for your children, your children's children, and for all who come after you, as one of the great sights which every American...should see."
—Teddy Roosevelt

Two Grand Canyon points were named for artists: Thomas Moran and Gunnar Widforss. Moran became rich and famous for his canyon paintings, one of which hangs in

---

Both rims are bordered by the Kaibab National Forest.

the U. S. Capitol building. The Swedish-born Widforss, who painted the canyon in the 1920s and 1930s, never got much attention or money. But to this day many other canyon artists say that Widforss was one of the best. His admirers in the National Park Service named a North Rim point and trail for him.

Q. What's the highest Grand Canyon overlook?
A. On the South Rim it's Navajo Point at 7,498 feet (2,285 m). But the top of the Desert View Watchtower is a bit taller. On the North Rim it's Point Imperial at 8,803 feet (2,683 m).

For the christening of the Yavapai Observation Station in 1928, park rangers wanted to have some Colorado River water. Ranger-naturalist Eddie McKee obtained the water, but the bottle broke before the ceremony. Secretly, McKee filled another bottle with tap water and stirred in mud.

Q. Of visitors to Grand Canyon National Park, what percent goes to the North Rim?
   A) 10 percent   B) 25 percent   C) 50 percent
A. A) 10 percent. Because of its higher elevation the North Rim gets far more snow than the South Rim, so North Rim facilities are open only five months a year, from May to October. The North Rim is also farther from cities and a major highway.

Q. How much snow falls on the North Rim in an average year?
A) 59 inches (150 cm)   B) 83 inches (210 cm)   C) 140 inches (355 cm)
A. C) 140 inches (355 cm). That's more than 11 feet of snow, enough to bury a house. The record snowfall was 272 inches (691 cm). The National Park Service keeps personnel on the North Rim all winter just to shovel snow off roofs. By contrast, Anchorage, Alaska, gets 83 inches, and Denver gets "only" 59 inches.

Q. Grand Canyon Lodge on the North Rim was built by the Union Pacific Railroad. How many trains used to arrive there every day?
   A) 100   B) 10   C) Zero

It has snowed on the canyon rim in July.

A. C) Zero. The railroad was 100 miles (160 km) away from the North Rim. The landscapes of southern Utah were too rugged for railroads. But the Union Pacific did run bus tours to the North Rim and to Utah parks like Bryce Canyon and Zion.

Q. Of all the visitors who visit the South Rim today, what percent arrives by train?

   A) 5 percent   B) 25 percent   C) 40 percent

A. A) 5 percent. When the Santa Fe Railway first built its tracks to the South Rim in 1901, almost all canyon visitors came by train. As automobiles and highways became more common, train traffic decreased until in 1968 train service to the canyon stopped. But two decades later the Grand Canyon Railway reopened; it brings more than 200,000 visitors every year, more than 1,000 a day in the summer.

Q. In 1920, 84 percent of canyon visitors came by train rather than car. By 1950 only 9 percent came by train. What was the last year that a majority of visitors came by train?

   A) 1926   B) 1932   C) 1940

A. A) 1926.

Q. What is unique about the Grand Canyon Railroad depot?

   A) It's the only railroad station inside a national park
   B) It's the only active railroad station in America made primarily of logs
   C) Both of the above.

A. C) Both of the above.

Q. The Santa Fe Railway had a subsidiary called the Fred Harvey Company, which built quality hotels and restaurants along the Santa Fe line. They also built most of the tourist facilities on the South Rim. Fred Harvey was an Englishman who was dismayed by the poor services along America's western railways. His restaurants were noted for their Harvey Girl waitresses. What famous movie was made about the Fred Harvey Company?

About 1,500 employees live on the South Rim year-round.

A. *The Harvey Girls* in 1946, starring Judy Garland, who sang the hit song The Atchison, Topeka, and the Santa Fe.

Q. Many Harvey Girls didn't work for Fred Harvey for very long. Why was this?
   A) Low wages   B) The West was too rough   C) They got married
A. C) They got married. Around 1900, men far outnumbered women in the West. Lonely men flocked to Fred Harvey restaurants to meet the pretty, educated, and respectable young Harvey Girls. Many Harvey Girls married leading citizens and founded some of the most prominent families of the Southwest. Soon eastern women with a taste for adventure were heading west to be Harvey Girls and to find husbands. The Fred Harvey Company had to stipulate in their contracts that they couldn't get married for one year.

Eight buildings at the Grand Canyon were designed by architect Mary Colter early in the 20th century. Colter had a genius for designing buildings that seemed to grow naturally out of the rocky landscape, such as Hermits Rest and Lookout Studio. She was also a great admirer of Native Americans and built Hopi House and the Desert View Watchtower as tributes to Native American culture. Two of her other creations, Phantom Ranch and the Bright Angel Lodge, were done in American frontier style. She also built two employee residence halls. In an era when women weren't allowed to be architects, the Santa Fe Railway realized that Colter had an inspired vision of how buildings could do justice to Southwestern landscapes and cultures, and the Santa Fe gave her the freedom, the authority, and the resources she needed to create enduring works of genius.

Q. El Tovar Hotel at Grand Canyon National Park and Old Faithful Inn at Yellowstone National Park are two of the most famous lodges of the American West. Which was built first?
A. Old Faithful Inn opened in 1904, El Tovar in 1905. Both were built by railroads. The Santa Fe Railway saw the success of the Northern Pacific Railway at developing tourism in Yellowstone and wanted to do the same for the Grand Canyon. The Santa Fe was determined to outdo the Northern Pacific and spent $250,000

About 400 employees live on the North Rim in the summer.

on El Tovar, compared with $140,000 for Old Faithful Inn. El Tovar was high tech for its time, with electric lights, running hot water, and steam heat. El Tovar produced its own fresh food with vegetable gardens, diary cows, and chickens.

Q. True or false: El Tovar Hotel has one of the fanciest dining rooms in any national park, but sometimes wild animals run through it.
A. True. Ringtails, which are like raccoons, get into the attic of El Tovar. They are tolerated because they keep the mice under control. Occasionally a ringtail will walk the rafters over the dining room even as people are dining.

Q. Inside the lobby of El Tovar Hotel there are two mounted moose heads. How many moose live in Grand Canyon National Park?
   A) 5,000   B) 200   C) Zero
A. C) Zero. There never were any moose in Grand Canyon National Park. The hotel just wanted to look like a 1900 hunting lodge. Some people may try to tell you that President Teddy Roosevelt shot these moose when he visited the Grand Canyon.

The first hotel on the North Rim consisted of a cluster of tent-cabins built in 1917 near today's Grand Canyon Lodge. It was built by W. W. Wylie, who had built similar tent-cabins at Yellowstone National Park.

Q. In 1911-1912 the Kolb brothers ran the Grand Canyon in boats and made a film of their adventures. In 1915 they began showing this film in their studio on the South Rim. How many years would they show this film?
   A) 20 years   B) 45 years   C) 61 years
A. C) 61 years. Emery Kolb showed it over 50,000 times, right until his death at age 95 in 1976. According to the Guinness Book of World Records, this is the longest running movie in world history. Hollywood star Douglas Fairbanks came to see it five times, and declared: "I consider it one of our best shows...because it's real." To advertise their movie, the Kolb brothers put up a sign saying: "Shooting the Rapids of the

---

In 1925 only 7,000 tourists visited the North Rim...

Colorado River." One day a lady saw this sign and protested: "Why would anyone want to shoot cute little bunny rabbits?"

Q. How many photographs did the Kolb brothers take at the Grand Canyon?
  A) 10,000   B) 500,000   C) 1.5 million
A. C) Late in his life Emery Kolb estimated that they had taken 1.5 million photos. Most photos were of mule riders, but the Kolbs also photographed remote parts of the canyon no one had ever photographed before.

Q. What 1930s New Deal program built many of the roads, walkways, viewpoints, retaining walls, and National Park Service buildings at the Grand Canyon and many other national parks?
  A) The CIA   B) The CBS   C) The CCC
A. C) The CCC. The Civilian Conservation Corps was a Great Depression program that gave jobs to young men, supported their families back home, and did major construction projects in national parks, work still visible today. At the Grand Canyon they built the Clear Creek Trail, the River Trail, and a telephone line across the canyon. There is a monument to the CCC at Hopi Point.

Q. The cemetery on the South Rim holds 300 graves. Who is buried there?
A. The cemetery is like a Grand Canyon history book. It holds pioneers like John Hance, Bill and Ada Bass, and the Kolb brothers, and also park rangers, Harvey Girls, and mule wranglers.

Epitaphs on tombstones in the Grand Canyon cemetery:

"They met and fell in love while working at the canyon."
"They shared a love of natural history and the Grand Canyon."
"His spirit is everywhere in the canyon he loved."
"He fell wholly in love with this Timeless Wonder, this Grand Canyon, calling it 'The place for us for all time.'"
"Just an old Harvey Girl at rest in the place she loved."
"John was well traveled. When he came to the Grand Canyon, he found home."
"Professor of the mule college."

...Today it's about half a million.

"Superintendent of Wrangell-St. Elias National Park. Started as a laborer at Grand Canyon National Park and worked his way to the top."
"Driver of the Grand Canyon stage. He left something of himself with everyone he met."
"Lost his life on geological river exploration of Colorado River."
"Nevermore" [a raven-loving ranger].

Q. True or false: There is a bridge that spans the entire Grand Canyon.
A. True. But it's only four miles (6.4 km) from the start of the Grand Canyon at Lees Ferry, so the canyon is only 800 feet (243 m) wide there. When Navajo Bridge was opened in 1929 it was the world's highest steel arch bridge at 470 feet (143 m) above the Colorado River. In 1995 a wider bridge was opened next to it, leaving the old bridge as a pedestrian walkway.

Q. Where does the drinking water at the Grand Canyon come from?
A. Water has always been in short supply on the canyon rims. When the Santa Fe Railway built the first hotels on the South Rim, they brought in all the water by train. They also built a pioneering water reclamation system. Today, water is pumped up from a natural spring, Roaring Springs, 3,000 feet (914 m) below the North Rim. This water runs through a pipeline that cost $6 million in 1966, and which was the largest helicopter-supported construction project in American history at that time. When the pipeline was nearly finished, a flash flood down Bright Angel Creek tore it apart, and it had to be rebuilt. This pipeline is only for water used inside the park; the hotels outside the South Rim park boundary rely on their own wells.

Grand Canyon Village is so isolated that it long had its own powerhouse, which blew a steam whistle every noon. When tourists asked what the whistle was, locals told them it was a steamboat pulling up to dock on the Colorado River. Some tourists went to the rim to look. A few swore they saw the steamboat.

When El Tovar Hotel opened in 1905, rooms cost $4, dinner $1.50.

Q. What's the best place to watch sunset or sunrise?
A. Grand Canyon sunrises and sunsets aren't about seeing the sun; they are about seeing the light effects on the canyon walls. The best views are looking away from the sun. Most overlooks work well for this. To see the whole drama, start at least an hour before sunset, and stay awhile after sunrise.

Q. How many scenic aircraft flights go over Grand Canyon every year?
    A) 5,000   B) 25,000   C) 90,000
A. C) 90,000.

Q. The Grand Canyon Skywalk is a horseshoe-shaped, glass-floored walkway that juts out over the canyon. Who built the Skywalk?
    A) The National Park Service   B) A Las Vegas Casino
               C) The Hualapai Indian Tribe
A. C) The Hualapai Tribe. The Skywalk was modeled after a Las Vegas attraction. It is a 250-mile (400 km) drive from Grand Canyon Village. The Skywalk is an important source of income for the Hualapais.

Q. Updrafts of warm air from the inner canyon to the rims are important because:
    A) They enable birds to glide for hours
    B) They promote condensation and rain
    C) They give the North Rim a more hospitable climate
    D) All of the above
A. D) All of the above. The updrafts even allowed the Ancestral Puebloans to grow corn at more than 8,000 feet (2,438 m) in elevation, an unusually high altitude for corn.

Q. Why are there forests on the canyon rim? Isn't Arizona supposed to be a desert?
A. It all depends on elevation. The bottom of the canyon is a desert with cactus, scorpions, and rattlesnakes. The elevation at the bottom of the canyon is similar to Tucson, and so is the temperature. The rim is a mile higher, and rainy enough to support forests. But these are still high-desert trees, adapted to survive on much less moisture than forests in wetter climates like the Pacific Northwest.

El Tovar was named for an officer of the Coronado expedition.

Q. What kinds of trees make up the rim forests?
A. The big, tall trees are ponderosa pines, part of the largest ponderosa forest in North America, stretching from the North Rim to southern New Mexico. The smaller, gnarly-looking trees are a mixture of pinyon pines and junipers. Notice how as you travel around the South Rim you go from zones of ponderosa trees to zones of only pinyons and junipers. A little elevation change makes a big difference. Ponderosas need more coolness and moisture and deeper soil, and here they are right at the boundary of where ponderosas can or can't grow.

Q. There are places on the South Rim where ponderosa trees grow a few hundred feet from the rim, but not on the rim itself. Why?
A. The warm air rising from the inner canyon dries them out too much. But pinyon and juniper trees, which can deal with drier climates, do grow along the rim.

Q. The bark of some ponderosa trees is reddish-orange, while on others it is black. What's the difference?
A. Younger ponderosas are darker. As ponderosas reach 150-200 years of age, they turn cinnamon colored.

Q. How old can ponderosas get?
   A) 100 years   B) 250 years   C) 500 years
A. C) 500 years, or more. The oldest known ponderosa, found in Colorado, was 1,047 years old.

Q. How long are the roots of ponderosa trees?
   A) 10 feet (3 m)   B) 50 feet (15 m)   C) 100 feet (30 m)
A. C) 100 feet (30 m). In a dry region, plants need to tap all the moisture they can reach.

Q. If you place your nose near the trunk of a ponderosa and sniff, what do ponderosas smell like?
   A) Vanilla   B) Butterscotch
A. You'll have to answer this one for yourself. The vanilla faction and the butterscotch faction have been arguing for years. Even the rangers don't agree.

In 1915 a horse-drawn buggy ride on the Hermit Road cost $3.

Q. On older, taller ponderosa trees the lowest branches may be 24 feet (7 m) or more above the ground. Why so high?
A. In a natural forest, forest fires often stay near the ground, burning ground cover, shrubs, and small trees. Taller trees can avoid being damaged by these low fires if their limbs are high enough. In addition to that adaptation to fire, Ponderosas have thick bark that resists fires.

Q. Are forest fires a danger at the Grand Canyon?
A. A big danger. Decades of human impacts, especially fire suppression, have allowed forests to become unnaturally dense all over the American West. In a natural ponderosa forest, frequent ground fires kill off smaller trees, leaving only larger trees. When white pioneers first arrived in northern Arizona they said that they could ride a horse through ponderosa forests. Today many areas, such as the Grandview area on the South Rim, are so thick with trees that a person can't even walk far. These overgrown forests almost guarantee catastrophic wildfires.

Q. What causes the most forest fires at the Grand Canyon?
   A) Lightning   B) Campfires   C) Cigarettes
A. A) Lightning. The Colorado Plateau receives more lightning than most areas on Earth. Today, if naturally ignited fires remain within safety limits, the National Park Service allows them to burn. The National Park Service also sets it own prescribed burns to reduce fuel loads in the forests and to mimic natural fire ecology.

Q. In a 35-year period (1940 to 1975), how many forest fires were caused by lightning in the American Southwest?
   A) 52,518   B) 15,102   C) 5,730
A. A) 52,518. That's an average of 1,500 fires every year, or more than 4 per day.

Q. Pinyon and juniper trees are usually mixed together, and are called a "pinyon-juniper forest," or "P-J" for short. How do you tell the two trees apart?
A. Pinyons are somewhat taller, up to 30 feet (9 m), while junipers seldom top 20 feet (6 m). Pinyons have needles (or 'pins'),

About 200 tree species live at the Grand Canyon.

while juniper leaves are more scale-like. Pinyons have cones with nut-like seeds, while junipers have berries. Juniper trunks look more gnarly and have bark that peels off in string-like pieces.

Q. The pinyon pine depends on one bird, the pinyon jay, to spread its seeds. The jays cache seeds far and wide, and their keen memories allow them to find most of their caches. The trees, of course, are counting on the jays to forget a few seeds. How many seeds can a pinyon jay carry in its mouth at one time?
  A) 10   B) 25   C) 50
A. C) 50 seeds.

Q. What advantage do seed caches give pinyon jays?
A. Because of their seed caches, pinyon jays can begin breeding earlier in the year than most birds, which have to wait for spring to create a food supply.

Q. The pinyon pine seed, also called a nut, is an incredibly rich source of nutrition. Pinyon nuts were an important food source for Ancestral Puebloans, and still are for Native Americans today. Pinyon nuts can be ground into flour to make pancakes. Which has more calories: a pound of pinyon nuts or a pound of Hershey's chocolate?
A. A pound of pinyon nuts has 2,800 calories, and a pound of Hershey's chocolate has 2,460 calories. And the fat in pinyon nuts is the good type of fat. But it isn't easy for pinyon trees to produce such nutritional wealth. Only every 5 to 7 years will the right growing conditions allow them to produce a bumper crop of nuts.

Q. True or false: Grand Canyon tourists sometimes eat deer poop.
A. You read that right deer dung. And it's true. But only by mistake. Deer poop is small pellets just about the same size, shape, and color as pinyon nuts. Some tourists pick up deer poop thinking they are picking up pinyon nuts. One way to double-check is to look up and see if there is actually a pinyon tree above the pinyon nuts. If not, don't swallow them!

Pinyon-juniper forests make up about 8 percent of the park.

Q. While pinyon nuts are quickly harvested by birds, animals, and humans, there are often plenty of juniper berries left on the trees. Why?
A. They have a bitter taste. Some young birds have been seen gobbling up juniper berries only to spit them out. But grey foxes like juniper berries.

Q. How long can juniper trees live?
   A) 100 years   B) 500 years   C) 1,400 years
A. C) Up to 1,400 years. Their companion tree, the pinyon pines, can live about 400 years.

Q. In the North Rim forests, Douglas fir trees are mixed with ponderosas, but on the South Rim, Douglas firs grow only in cliff alcoves just below the rim. Why?
A. The Douglas firs require high elevations, coolness, and lots of moisture. The South Rim is too low and warm for them. But north-facing alcoves are shady and often retain snow, so Douglas firs can grow there.

Q. In the Ice Age, Douglas firs grew inside the canyon, far below where they grow today. How far down in the canyon did they grow?
   A) 1,000 feet (304 m)   B) 2,000 feet (609 m)
              C) 3,000 feet (914 m)
A. C) 3,000 feet (914 m). Several species of plants, and one snail species, that were widespread in the canyon in the Ice Age now barely survive at scattered springs.

Q. The North Rim holds groves of aspen trees. How are aspens different from other Grand Canyon forest trees?
   A) White bark
   B) Golden-yellow leaves in autumn
   C) Reproduces not by seeds, but by roots sending out new shoots
   D) All of the above
A. D) All of the above.

Q. Just east of Desert View there is Cedar Mountain, and on the South Kaibab Trail there's Cedar Mesa and Cedar Ridge. What kind of cedar trees grow there?

There are Joshua trees in the western Grand Canyon.

A. None. The first pioneers in the area thought they were seeing cedar trees, but the trees are really junipers.

Q. From both the South Rim and the North Rim you can see patches of trees at Indian Garden, and from some overlooks you can see trees at Phantom Ranch. What kind of trees are these?

A. Mostly cottonwood trees. Cottonwoods can grow in deserts, but they require an abundant water supply. Unlike most desert plants, cottonweed leaves are poor at conserving water. For pioneer travelers in the West, cottonwood groves were a welcome sight. For birds they offer excellent nesting hollows.

Q. How did cottonwood trees get their name?

A. Cottonwoods got their name because their seeds are attached to little cotton-like parachutes, which fly far on the wind.

Q. A shrub found on the South Rim is the skunk bush. How did it get its name?

       A) It smells bad   B) Skunks love it
             C) It's black with white stripes

A. A) It smells bad. But its berries make a good lemonade-like drink.

Q. A common shrub found on the rims is sagebrush. If you rub a leaf with your fingers, it gives off a pungent smell, but this isn't the same sage used as a food seasoning. The sagebrush is a common sight on western plains. What famous Western novel used sage in its title?

A. Zane Grey's *Riders of the Purple Sage*, published in 1912. Zane Grey explored the Grand Canyon over many years and included it in several novels.

Q. Agaves and yuccas are plants with thick, bayonet-like leaves. They look similar, but agave leaves are lined with sharp teeth, and yucca leaves with curling fibers. These fibers are so strong that Native Americans used them to make sandals and ropes, yet so thin that they could be used as paintbrushes for painting

Mather Point originally had three balanced rocks...

pottery. By mashing and soaking the roots of yuccas in water, what did Native Americans make?

A) Soup   B) Soap and shampoo   C) Jelly

A. B) Soap and Shampoo. One species of yucca is even called the soaptree yucca.

Q. Pioneers originally called the agave 'the century plant' because they supposed it bloomed only once in a century. In reality, how often does it bloom?

A) 200 years   B) 30 years   C) 5 years

A. B) 30 years, on average. To flower, an agave sends up a flower stalk that can be twice as tall as a person and which can grow 10 inches (25 cm) a day.

Q. Why were Native Americans so alert to the flowering of agave plants?

A. Just before the flower stalk arises, agaves are loaded with sugars. Native Americans waited until just before agaves sent up their flower stalks, then harvested the plants, placed them in pits made of big piles of rock, and roasted them. For desert tribes, agaves were essential to survival. The Grand Canyon holds hundreds of roasting pits from centuries ago.

Ponderosa forests make up about 2 percent of Grand Canyon National Park.

About 10 percent of Grand Canyon plant species are exotics, introduced by human actions.

You don't want to test out how the catclaw acacia got its name.

There was once a South Rim rock formation called "the duck on the rock," but around the year 2000 its head fell off.

...In the 1990s, one slid off.

THE RIVER

Q. The Colorado River was named for:
   A) Its color   B) The state of Colorado   C) The Colorado Plateau
A. A) Its color. Spanish explorers named it the Rio Colorado, Spanish for Red River. The river was red because of the huge amount of silt it carried. Today all of that silt is trapped behind Glen Canyon Dam, so the river is usually green. Only when rainstorms start side streams that empty into the river does the river look red or brown.

Q. How many square miles does the Colorado River (including its tributaries) drain?
   A) 44,000 (112,820 sq km)   B) 144,000 (369,230 sq km)
      C) 244,000 (625,641 sq km)
A. C) 244,000 square miles (625,641 sq km), including almost all of Arizona and parts of six other states: Utah, Colorado, New Mexico, Wyoming, Nevada, and California.

Q. The Colorado River is 1,450 miles (2,333 km) long. What percent of the river's length lies inside the Grand Canyon?
   A) 9 percent   B) 19 percent   C) 39 percent
A. B) 19 percent.

Q. In length, how does the Colorado River rank among North American rivers?
   A) 1st   B) 6th   C) 10th
A. B) 6th. The Colorado River comes in behind the Mississippi River the longest at 2,340 miles (3,765 km) the Missouri, the Yukon, the Rio Grande, and the Arkansas.

Q. The Colorado River may be famous for its power at carving canyons and for its whitewater rapids, but this power is due more to gradient than to volume of water. On a list of North American rivers ranked by volume, where does the Colorado River rank?
   A) 5th   B) 10th   C) 27th

A. C) 27th. The Colorado River has only about 1/10th the volume of the Mississippi River, but it is 13 times steeper than the Mississippi and 17 times steeper within the Grand Canyon. The Colorado once carried 17 times more sediment than the Mississippi, sediment that helped carve the Grand Canyon.

Q. The Colorado River is very unusual for being a great river that flows through a desert. Another example is the Nile. Before Glen Canyon Dam was built, which river carried more sediment, the Colorado or the Nile?
A. The Colorado carried ten times more sediment than the Nile.

Q. Where does the Colorado River begin?
   A) Utah   B) Colorado   C) Wyoming   D) All of the above
A. D) All of the above. It used to begin at the junction of the Green and Grand rivers in Utah. But in 1921 Coloradoans decided that the Colorado River should begin in Colorado, so they got the Grand River renamed the Colorado. Now the Colorado River begins in Rocky Mountain National Park. But since the Green River is twice as long and drains twice the area of the former Grand River, some geographers feel that the Green River, which begins in Wyoming, should be considered the real source of the Colorado River.

> "There is an initial shock of astonishment as one catches a glimpse far below of the Colorado River, maker of Grand Canyon. Dwarfed by the depth, it almost escapes notice."
> —Edgar Lee Masters

Q. How deep is the Colorado River?
   A) 10 feet (3 m)   B) 18 feet (5.5 m)   C) 85 feet (26 m)
A. B) 18 feet (5.5 m) on average. The deepest spot measured by sonar is 85 feet (26 m), but other spots may top 100 feet (30 m).

Q. There are four deserts in North America, each with a distinct climate and ecosystem. As it flows through the Grand Canyon, how many of these deserts does the Colorado River encounter?
   A) 1   B) 2   C) 3

A. C) 3. For its first 40 miles (64 km) in the Grand Canyon, the Colorado River flows through a Great Basin Desert environment. From mile 40 to mile 150 (241 km), it's the Sonoran Desert. From mile 150 to mile 277 (445 km), it's the Mojave Desert.

Q. What temperature is the Colorado River?
A) 100 degrees (38 C)   B) 75 degrees (24 C)   C) 50 degrees (10 C)
A. C) About 50 degrees (10 C). The river was once a warm, desert river, but today it emerges from deep under Lake Powell at Glen Canyon Dam, just upstream from the Grand Canyon. At the dam the river water is 48 degrees, and it warms up about one degree for every 30 miles (48 km) it flows. The cold water adds to the danger for river runners because anyone thrown into the water risks hypothermia even with an air temperature of 120 degrees (49 C).

Q. True or false: The trout in the Colorado River rode to the bottom of the canyon on the backs of mules.
A. True. When Glen Canyon Dam changed the Colorado River into a cold-water river, it wiped out most of the native fish species, which were adapted to warm water. Trout, a cold-water species, were originally introduced into a few cool Grand Canyon side streams in the early 1900s for sport fishing. The trout were carried in canisters on the back of mules. When the river became cold, the trout spread into the river.

Q. Of the native Colorado River fish that were wiped out by the building of dams, the largest was the Colorado pike minnow, the largest minnow in North America, often called the Colorado River Salmon. How much did they weigh?
A) 30 pounds (13.6 kg)   B) 50 pounds (23 kg)   C) 80 pounds (36 kg)
A. C) 80 pounds (36 kg). They grew to 6 feet (2 m) long. To catch them, pioneer fishermen baited hooks with baby rabbits.

Q. The volume of rivers is usually measured in cubic feet per second (cfs). To visualize one cubic foot of water, imagine a basketball full of water. If you were standing on the shore of

---

the Colorado River, how many basketballs of water would you see going past you every second?

    A) 50   B) 1,000   C) 14,000

A. C) 14,000 basketballs every second. But this volume can vary quite a bit depending on how much water is being released from Glen Canyon Dam.

Q. Before Glen Canyon Dam stopped the Colorado River's spring floods, what was the highest flow ever recorded in the Grand Canyon?

    A) 75,000 cfs   B) 150,000 cfs   C) 210,000 cfs

A. C) 210,000, in June, 1884. That's 210,000 basketballs going past you every second. The average peak was 84,000 cfs. About once every ten years, the spring floods reached 120,000 cfs.

Q. What was the lowest flow ever recorded in the Grand Canyon?

    A) 5,000 cfs   B) 2,000 cfs   C) 700 cfs

A. C) 700 cfs in December, 1924. The lowest flows were always in the winter.

Q. In the spring flood of 1921, how many tons of silt was measured going past Phantom Ranch in one day?

    A) 100 tons   B) 10,000 tons   C) 27 million tons

A. C) 27 million tons in one day! That's like 6 million elephants stampeding past you in one day. And that's only the sediment in the water, not the water itself. The Colorado was one muddy river. On an average day, the river may have carried "merely" 168,000 tons of sediment. But this was before Glen Canyon Dam started trapping this sediment in Lake Powell. Without fresh silt, beaches in the Grand Canyon are disappearing. In 1996, 2004, 2008, and 2012, experimental floods were used to restore canyon beaches.

Q. Today the largest source of sediment for the Grand Canyon is the Paria River, which enters the Colorado River at Lees Ferry. The Paria River delivers about 1.5 million tons of silt into the Grand Canyon every year; by contrast, all the other side streams combined deliver only 290,000 tons of silt per year. The Paria River is so small that if it were back east, it would be called a creek. But the Paria drains a large desert area, so it has one of

---

The Powell expedition rowed 1/250th of the distance to the moon.

the highest concentrations of sediment of any river in the world. What percentage of the Paria's volume consists of silt?
  A) 10 percent   B) 25 percent   C) 50 percent
A. C) Nearly 50 percent.

Q. How many rapids are in the Grand Canyon?
  A) 50   B) 90   C) 160
A. C) There are 160 named rapids, but some of these diminish or disappear as the water level changes, and some unnamed riffles are larger than named rapids.

Q. As it flows through the Grand Canyon, the Colorado River drops about 2,000 feet (609 m) in elevation, but only 9 percent of the river's length in the canyon is made up of rapids. How much of the river's elevation drop is made by rapids?
  A) 9 percent   B) 20 percent   C) 50 percent
A. C) 50 percent. The Colorado River sometimes forms lazy pools, but at rapids it drops abruptly. It can drop 10 feet (3 m) or more in only seconds.

Q. What's the largest drop of any rapid in the Grand Canyon?
  A) 20 feet (6 m)   B) 25 feet (7.6 m)   C) 30 feet (9 m)
A. C) 30 feet (9 m) at Hance Rapid. Fortunately, this isn't 30 feet in one abrupt drop. But there are plenty of rapids that give rafters the feeling that they are plunging over waterfalls. There's a good reason why Lava Falls is called Lava Falls.

Q. What causes rapids in the Grand Canyon?
  A) Earthquakes   B) Landslides   C) Flash floods
A. C) Flash floods. Almost all the rapids are at the mouth of side canyons. When side streams flood they flush huge quantities of rock into the river, building a boulder dam, which the river has to flow over.

Q. When do flash floods occur in the Grand Canyon?
A. Most flash floods happen in the summer monsoon season, which starts around July 4th. Daily thunderstorms can dump inches of rain in a small area. You could be enjoying sunny skies in a side canyon, miles below where it is raining, and still be killed by a flash flood.

Great blue herons are a common sight along the Colorado River.

Q. How difficult are Grand Canyon rapids?
A. On most rivers, rapids are rated on a 1-6 scale, with a 6 being impassable. The Colorado River is unique for the size and power of its waves, and thus it has its own 1-10 scale. One vague rule is that the numbers correspond to the height of the waves: a '7' has 7-foot (2 m) waves. But waves can get much higher than 10 feet (3 m), and extra points are added for obstructions. While relatively few Grand Canyon rapids require serious maneuvering, boaters are always outmatched by the sheer power of the river. Even a straightforward wave train of 10-foot waves can flip a raft. The difficulty of most rapids varies with the river level, but the most formidable rapids, Crystal and Lava Falls, are always a '10.'

Q. What is a "blind drop?"
A. Blind drops are steep rapids where you can't see the layout of the rapid until the last second. If you've made a mistake about your entry, it's too late! The canyon's most difficult rapids, Crystal Rapid and Lava Falls, are among many blind drops.

Q. Which rapid has caused the most deaths?
A. Crystal Rapid, with 6 deaths.

Q. Who named Grand Canyon rapids?
A. Most were named by river runners, starting with John Wesley Powell in 1869. Some names commemorate river mishaps, such as Upset Rapid. Doris Rapid is where Doris Nevills was knocked into the river in 1940. Doris's middle name was actually 'Drown,' but she didn't drown. But 25-mile Rapid, informally called Hansbrough-Richards Rapid, was named for two men who did drown there in 1889.

Q. Henry Richards, for whom Hansbrough-Richards Rapid was named, was notable for something else. He was:
    A) The first African American to boat the Grand Canyon
    B) The grandfather of Keith Richards of the Rolling Stones
    C) Smarter than Peter Hansbrough
A. A and C. Richards was the first African American to boat the Grand Canyon, along with George Washington Gibson, both of whom were cooks on the 1889 Brown-Stanton expedition.

Two of Powell's crew, Oramel and Seneca Howland...

Richards thought it was foolish to run the rapid and wanted to lower the boats with ropes, but Peter Hansbrough insisted they run it.

Q. One Grand Canyon rapid was named for a U. S. president. Which president?
A) Teddy Roosevelt   B) John F. Kennedy   C) Warren Harding
A. C) Warren Harding. When President Harding died in office in 1923, an expedition of U.S. government surveyors and geologists was boating down the Colorado River. On their radio they heard about Harding's death, and they named a rapid for him.

Q. The Grand Canyon contains a creek and a rapid called Tuna. Does Tuna Creek have tuna fish in it?
A. No, tuna is the Spanish word for the fruit of the prickly pear cactus, which grows abundantly here.

Q. The Colorado River is so powerful that some of its eddies are named for the trouble they cause boaters. Forever eddy could keep a boat forever. Helicopter eddy could take a helicopter to get you out. The room of doom could be your end. On the other hand, there's Six-pack eddy. What's it famous for?
A. It collects river flotsam, including cans of soda and beer, that river runners have lost in the first 220 miles (353 km) of a Grand Canyon trip.

Five famous rapids you can see from the rim:
1. Hermit Rapid (seen from Hopi Point): Some of the largest waves in the canyon, 10 to 15 feet (3-4.5 m) high. The wave train is straight but steep enough to flip 18-foot (5.4 m) rafts.
2. Granite Rapid (from Pima Point): Forced up against a granite cliff, waves are much more chaotic than Hermit Rapid.
3. Hance Rapid (from Moran and Lipan points): The steepest total drop in the Grand Canyon, and the rockiest. Boaters face serious maneuvering. Boats stuck on rocks have required helicopters to free them.
4. Unkar Rapid (from Lipan Point, and Cape Royal on the North Rim): Not as formidable as the first three, but perhaps the most beautiful, a long wave train beneath

---

...were descended from a Mayflower pilgrim.

red cliffs. If you see rafts tied up on the right shore, river runners are exploring the Ancestral Puebloan ruins on the Unkar Creek Delta, where the Puebloans farmed.

5. Lava Falls (from Toroweap, a 3-4 hour drive west of North Rim facilities): One of the most famous rapids in the world. The river plunges over volcanic boulders, creating huge, chaotic waves and hydraulics. Even 30-foot (9 m) motorized rafts have flipped here.

Joke: River guides say that there are two kinds of river guides in the Grand Canyon: those who have already been flipped by the Colorado River, and those who are going to be flipped.

Q. Why was John Wesley Powell, the leader of the first Colorado River expedition, an unusually brave man?
   A) He fought bravely in the Civil War
   B) He had only one arm and thus couldn't swim
   C) No one knew if it was even possible to take boats down the Colorado River
   D) All of the above
A. D) All of the above. Powell fought at the battle of Shiloh and lost his arm. For all he knew, there could have been an impassable waterfall that would had left him trapped at the bottom of the canyon.

Q. How much experience did Powell and his crew have at running whitewater rivers?
   A) None   B) Years   C) A few rivers
A. A) None at all. Powell and his men had to learn everything along the way. One of the first things they learned was that their heavy wooden boats, which were designed for lakes, were a bad design for whitewater. (You can see replicas of Powell's boats outside the IMAX theater just outside the South Rim park boundary.)

Until Navajo Bridge, Lees Ferry was the only Colorado River ...

"We are now ready to start our way down the Great Un-known...We are three quarters of a mile in the depths of the earth, and the great river shrinks into insignificance, as it dashes its angry waves against the walls and cliffs, that rise to the world above; they are but puny riffles, and we but pygmies, running up and down the sands, or lost among the boulders. We have an unknown distance yet to run; an unknown river to explore. What falls there are, we know not; what rocks beset the channel, we know not; what walls rise over the river, we know not."
—John Wesley Powell

Q. Some of the most prominent buttes visible from the South Rim are named Sumner, Dunn, Howland, Bradley, and Hall. What do these names have in common?
A. They were the names of John Wesley Powell's boatmen on his 1869 Colorado River expedition.

Q. When John Wesley Powell landed at the mouth of the Little Colorado River, which is a side canyon of the Grand Canyon, he found an Ancestral Puebloan ruin there. Later visitors found no ruin, only a stone cabin built by prospector Ben Beamer. What happened to the ruin?
A. Beamer used its stones to build his cabin.

Q. True or false: A steamboat explored the Colorado River a decade before the Powell expedition.
A. True. In 1858 Joseph Ives led the first U.S. government expedition to explore the Grand Canyon region. Ives built a special steamboat and sailed up the Colorado River from the Gulf of California. He spent two months going upstream until his boat wrecked on a rock, far short of the Grand Canyon. Ives then headed overland and descended into the Grand Canyon at Diamond Creek. Accompanying Ives were two German artists, the first artists to portray the Grand Canyon.

Q. How many people raft through the Grand Canyon every year?
  A) 1,000   B) 10,000   C) 25,000
A. C) About 25,000.

...road crossing for 440 miles (707 km).

Six Grand Canyon river pioneers:
1. John Wesley Powell led the first Grand Canyon expedition in 1869.
2. Amos Burg ran the first rubber raft through the Grand Canyon in 1938.
3. Norm Nevills started commercial river running in 1938.
4. Alexander Zee Grant ran the first kayak through the Grand Canyon in 1941.
5. Georgie White Clark started the first company to use rubber rafts in 1952.
6. Martin Litton started running wooden dories in the Grand Canyon in 1964. He also helped save Grand Canyon river running by preventing two dams from being built inside the canyon in the 1960s.

Q. Has anyone done a solo boat trip through the Grand Canyon?
A. Buzz Holmstrom worked as a gas station attendant in Oregon, but he was a brilliant boat builder and boatman. In 1937 he ran the Colorado River by himself. Holmstrom found that being alone allowed him to pay more attention to the magic of the canyon, which he wrote about poetically in his journal. Since then, a few people have done solo trips in rafts or kayaks.

Q. True or false: To kayak the Grand Canyon, you have to be a young, super athlete.
A. False. In 1987 a 73-year-old man named Spike White, who ran a summer camp in the Missouri Ozarks, kayaked the length of the Grand Canyon. He had started kayaking only three years before, at age 70. When White made it through Lava Falls without flipping, his companions lifted his kayak on their shoulders, with White still in it, and gave him a victory parade up the beach.

Q. Who were the first women to boat the Grand Canyon?
A. In 1872 John Wesley Powell's sister Nellie ran the canyon's first rapid. In 1923 Edith Kolb met her father Emery at Hance Rapid, one of the most dangerous, when Emery was guiding a U.S. Geological Survey trip. After running Hance Rapid, Edith went back up the Hance Trail. In 1928 Bessie Hyde and her husband Glenn ran most of the Grand Canyon on a honeymoon

In migration season, unusual birds pause along the river, even pelicans.

trip, but they didn't finish the whole trip. In 1938 the first commercial river trip through the Grand Canyon, led by Norm Nevills, included two women: Elzada Clover was a botanist from the University of Michigan and Lois Jotter was her student.

Q. Women who row rafts in the Grand Canyon sometimes lack the muscle power of male boaters, but in one respect, this actually makes them better boaters. Why is this?
A. The Colorado River is so powerful that no one not even an Olympic weight lifter can out-muscle it. The best guides are those who best understand the dynamics of the currents and waves, and can make the river work for them, not against them. Women guides are sometimes better at getting along with the river.

Q. What's the speed record for rowing a boat through the Grand Canyon? (Starting at Lees Ferry and going through 235 miles of rapids).
   A) 36 hours   B) 72 hours   C) 100 hours
A. A) 36 hours, set by three veteran river guides in a wooden dory in the unusually high water of 1983. A normal rowing trip takes two weeks.

Q. What's the speed record for a kayaker?
   A) 36 hours   B) 49 hours   C) 100 hours
A. B) 49 hours, set in 1978 by Fletcher Anderson on a solo trip.

Q. Did anyone ever swim through the Grand Canyon?
A. In 1955 two hardcore California surfers, Bill Beer and John Daggett, wore wetsuits and lifejackets and clung to waterproof gear bags to swim the length of the canyon. It took them 26 days, a few cuts and bruises, and, they admitted afterward, perhaps lots of foolishness.

> "If you want to lose a man, let him think he is better than that river."
> —Bert Loper, river runner

Q. How did the Grand Canyon launch the political career of Senator Barry Goldwater?
A. Barry Goldwater was the son of a famous Arizona trading

Powell's expedition lasted 100 days and 1,000 miles (1,609 km).

post and department store family. In 1940 he took a trip down the Colorado River. He was one of the first 100 people ever to run the Grand Canyon. He turned his photos and film into a public lecture and toured Arizona with it. This tour made him a well-known figure and launched his career in politics.

Q. True or false: The crew of one early Grand Canyon river trip included a black bear.
A. True. When Clyde Eddy went down the river in 1927 he took along a black bear cub named Cataract, and a dog named Rags. Cataract and Rags loved to play with one another in camp, but they weren't always so happy about going through rapids. In one rapid, Cataract was knocked out of the boat. But he managed to cling to its railing.

Q. Virginia Rice was one of the unluckiest passengers to go down the Colorado River. In 1996 her raft flipped in Lava Falls. She swam to shore and climbed out. What happened next?
A. A rattlesnake bit her twice! She had to be helicoptered out of the canyon, but she lived.

Three famous Grand Canyon river mysteries:
1. In 1867 a starving and delirious man, James White, washed up on a log raft below the Grand Canyon. Ever since, river buffs have debated whether White really came all the way through the Grand Canyon.
2. Near the end of John Wesley Powell's 1869 expedition three of his crew members left the river and headed for Mormon towns. They disappeared without a trace. Some say Indians killed them, some say Mormons.
3. In 1928 Glenn and Bessie Hyde took a honeymoon boat trip through the Grand Canyon. Their boat was found abandoned in the lower canyon, still full of gear, but there was no trace of them.

Q. As late as the 1960s the Bureau of Reclamation was planning to build two dams inside the Grand Canyon. What percent of the Grand Canyon's length would the dams have flooded?
A) 10 percent   B) 25 percent   C) 50 percent
A. C) 50 percent. The dams would have put an end to river

Most of Powell's crew were Civil War veterans, accustomed to hardship.

running and flooded many of the canyon's most famous features. Only a Sierra Club-led campaign stopped the dams and just barely.

Q. Much of the green zone alongside the Colorado River consists of tamarisk, a tree brought from the Middle East to America in the late 1800s. Tamarisks quickly spread up river corridors throughout the Southwest, crowding out native plants. Tamarisk consumes enormous amounts of water, depleting limited water supplies in springs and creeks. It spreads fast because it produces enormous numbers of seeds. How many seeds does one tamarisk plant produce every year?

A) 6,000 seed   B) 160,000   C) 600,000
A. C) 600,000 seeds.

Most Colorado River water is snowmelt from the Rocky Mountains; little of its water comes from the deserts of Arizona, Nevada, and California.

In volume the Colorado River is about equal to the Delaware River, but it has far more human demands upon it, more than it can handle.

Rowing the Grand Canyon is the Mt. Everest of river trips, but unlike Everest, infamous for climber's garbage, canyon beaches are kept pristine.

John Wesley Powell became head of the U.S. Geological Survey.

In 1871-1872 Powell led a second Colorado River expedition, but he finished it barely half way through the Grand Canyon and hiked out.

The Colorado River is diverted for so many human uses, it no longer reaches the sea.

Mesquite trees along the river are up to 750 years old.

THE TRAILS

Q. How many miles of hiking trails are in the Grand Canyon?
   A) 50 miles (80 km)   B) 260 (415 km)   C) 350 (530 km)
A. C) About 260 miles (415 km). But only 31 miles (50 km) are regularly maintained by the National Park Service; much of the rest has been abandoned for nearly a century. There's another 30 miles (48 km) of trails along the rim.

Q. Who built the hiking trails in the Grand Canyon?
   A) Native Americans   B) Miners   C) The National Park Service   D) All of the above.
A. D) All of the above. Large animals like deer and bighorn sheep needed to get in and out of the canyon, or down to the river, to find food and water. They found the easiest routes. Then Native Americans arrived and followed the game animals. When Native Americans started living inside the canyon, they wore better trails for humans. When white miners arrived, they needed trails good enough for pack animals. Most of today's trails were originally mining trails. The National Park Service built the South Kaibab Trail. The CCC built the Clear Creek Trail and the River Trail. The National Park Service has continued improving the two main trails, the Kaibab and Bright Angel, but others are slowly decaying.

Q. Of the 8 trails that go off the South Rim, how many were named for the early prospectors who built the trails?
   A) 2   B) 5   C) 8
A. B) 5. The Bass, Hance, Tanner, Hermit, and Boucher trails.

Q. The Bright Angel Trail was once a private toll trail. If you used it in 1909, how much would it have cost?
   A) 50 cents   B) $1   C) $20
A. B) One dollar, if you were riding a mule or horse. Of course, when you add a century of inflation, that's more than $20 in today's money.

There are several unique things about the South Kaibab Trail:

1. Most trails follow old animal and Native American trails, but the South Kaibab was a new route, dynamited out of sheer cliffs.
2. It's the only trail built by the National Park Service, which wanted an alternative to the private Bright Angel Trail.
3. Most trails stay inside side canyons, but the South Kaibab Trail runs along ridgelines, offering better views of the canyon. This makes it much hotter in the summer.
4. It's the shortest route to the Colorado River, 6.3 miles (10.1 km). This means it's also the steepest route.

Q. How much did the South Kaibab Trail cost to build in 1925?
   A) One million dollars   B) Five million dollars   C) $73,000
A. C) Only $73,000. In today's dollars this is less than a million dollars and still a bargain.

Q. If you were on the South Kaibab Trail in 1928 you might have seen dozens of Havasupai Indians carrying a long, one-ton steel cable on their shoulders, snaking it down the trail. What were they doing?
A. Carrying down cable to build the black suspension bridge that crosses the Colorado River to Phantom Ranch. When this bridge was completed, it was the only bridge across the Colorado River for 755 miles (1,214 km).

Q. Before the footbridges were built at Phantom Ranch, how did tourists get across the Colorado River?
A. On a crude cable tramway built in 1907. The horses and mules didn't like it one bit!

Q. What's the record for running across the Grand Canyon on the 21-mile (34 km) Kaibab Trail from the South Rim to the North Rim?
   A) 10 hours   B) 6 hours   C) 3 hours
A. C) 3 hours, set in 1981 by Allyn Cureton. Cureton also set the record for running 42 miles (68 km) rim-to-rim-to-rim: 7 hours, 51 minutes.

Park ranger Eddie McKee often hiked across the canyon...

Q. On the South Kaibab Trail you go from rocks 270 million years old at the rim to rocks 1.75 billion years old at the bottom of the canyon. With each footstep, how many years are you walking over?
   A) 1,000 years   B) 10,000 years C) 50,000 years
A. C) About 50,000 years with every footstep.

Q. How do employees at Phantom Ranch get in and out of the canyon?
A. They hike. They work 10-day shifts and have 4 days off, so this leaves enough time to get out and go places. Sometimes they will hike out in the evening to visit friends on the rim and hike back down again that same night, a 15-mile (24 km) round-trip.

Joke: The staff at Phantom Ranch can always tell which guests hiked down and which guests rode down on mules. The hikers don't want to stand up, and the mule riders don't want to sit down.

Q. True or false: There was once a cable tramway from the rim to the inner canyon.
A. True. To reach its tourist camp at the bottom of the Hermit Trail, the Santa Fe Railway built a 6,300-foot-long (1,902 m) tram to it in 1926. This was the longest single-span tram in America. It dropped 3,600 feet (1,097 m).

Q. What happened to Hermit Camp and the tramway?
A. Hermit Camp and the tramway were abandoned in 1930 after the National Park Service opened the free South Kaibab trail to Phantom Ranch. Tourists preferred Phantom Ranch because it was on the Colorado River.

Q. How long is the longest trail in the Grand Canyon?
   A) 21 miles (34 km)   B) 40 miles (64 km)   C) 95 miles (152 km)
A. C) 95 miles (152 km). The Tonto Trail follows the Tonto platform through one-third of the Grand Canyon. From most South Rim overlooks you can spot the Tonto Trail winding in and out of the drainages on the Tonto platform below. The word "Tonto" comes from the Tonto Apaches. Unfortunately, as with many names whites gave to Native Americans, this one seems to

---

...to date his future wife.

have been an insult, meaning "stupid." Then again, many hikers who travel the often shadless and waterless Tonto Trail in summer find that stupid is the perfect description of themselves.

Q. Pioneers Bill and Ada Bass lived on the South Rim and had a mine near the Colorado River. Occasionally, but only during the dry seasons, Ada packed her horse and made a 3-day trip down the Bass Trail to the river and back. What was she doing?
A. The laundry.

Q. Who was the first white woman to go down a South Rim trail into the Grand Canyon?
A. Emma Burbank Ayer, the wife of a Flagstaff lumberman. She went down the Hance Trail in 1885. Ayer Point, near the Hance Trail, was named in her honor.

Q. Which First Lady hiked up the Bright Angel Trail in the worst of the summer heat, after doing a river trip to Phantom Ranch?
   A) Hillary Clinton   B) Laura Bush   C) Jackie Kennedy
A. B) Laura Bush. And when her father-in-law George H. W. Bush was president, he hiked a mile down the South Kaibab Trail. President Bush was over 65 years old, and park rangers worried that the president might have a heart attack on the trail, but Bush did fine.

Q. In 1966 Senator Robert Kennedy hiked up the Bright Angel Trail in the summer heat after a river trip. To encourage his exhausted friends, what did Kennedy quote to them?
   A) The Little Engine That Could
   B) The song "Climb Every Mountain"
   C) Shakespeare
A. C) Shakespeare. Specifically, the St. Crispin's Day speech from Henry V, in which Henry V urged we band of brothers to bravery and great deeds in a coming battle.

When the Kolb brothers built their photography studio on the South Rim in 1901, they sometimes didn't have enough water to develop all the photos they took of mule riders. So they built a darkroom at Indian Garden, 4.5 miles (7 km) down the Bright Angel Trail. Indian Garden had plenty

The Tanner Trail was originally called the Horsethief Trail...

of water. After taking photos of mule riders starting down the trail, Emery Kolb carried his film down to the darkroom, developed the film, and then raced back up the trail before the riders returned. Sometimes Emery did two trips a day, or 18 miles (29 km).

Q. Has anyone hiked inside the Grand Canyon for its full length?
A. In 1976 a river guide named Kenton Grua took 36 days to hike from Lees Ferry to the Grand Wash Cliffs. This is 277 miles (445 km) by river, but a lot longer by foot. Grua was also one of the three river guides who set a river speed record of 36 hours in 1983.

Q. Harvey Butchart, a meek-looking math professor from Flagstaff, Arizona, became a legendary Grand Canyon hiker. Over four decades he pioneered numerous difficult routes no one had ever done before. How many total miles did Butchart hike in the canyon?
A) 2,000 miles (3,218 km)   B) 6,000 (9,654 km)   C) 12,000 (19,308 km)
A. C) 12,000 miles (19,308 km).

Q. What percent of Grand Canyon visitors go hiking overnight inside the canyon?
    A) 1 percent   B) 5 percent   C) 9 percent
A. A) About 1 percent, or over 50,000. A majority of these go to Phantom Ranch.

Q. What would be the best training for hiking in the Grand Canyon?
    A) Climbing Mt. Everest   B) Running a marathon
                C) Hiking in Death Valley
A. C) Hiking in Death Valley. The most valuable asset for Grand Canyon hikers is an understanding of a desert environment, especially the severe demands that heat and dryness place upon the human body. Many hikers with years of experience in the Rockies or Alps come to the Grand Canyon with dangerous overconfidence, without recognizing how different the Grand Canyon is from humid, stream-filled mountains.

...rustlers used it to take stolen horses into Arizona from Utah.

Q. Should a desert hiker be on the "shirts" team or "skins" team?
A. Shirts. The desert is like a giant vacuum cleaner sucking moisture out of the human body, and hikers often fail to carry, find, or drink enough water. They also make serious mistakes such as removing a t-shirt. Hiking without a shirt greatly increases evaporation from the torso and vital organs.

Q. Every year Grand Canyon hikers die or suffer horribly because they don't understand the desert's impact on the human body. A hiker will be dehydrated after losing how much body fluid?
    A) 2.5 percent   B) 10 percent   C) 15 percent
A. A) 2.5 percent. At 5 percent, a hiker becomes nauseous. By 10 percent, dizziness and headaches may be incapacitating. By 15 percent, death is imminent.

Q. Of hiking-related deaths, what percent are caused by heat stroke?
    A) 10 percent   B) 25 percent   C) 50 percent
A. C) 50 percent. Most other hiking deaths are due to heart attacks, which are often heat-induced.

Q. How do supplies get to Phantom Ranch?
    A) Helicopters   B) Mules   C) Boats
A. B) Almost everything goes in and out on the backs of mules. Some mule trains are for carrying riders, and others are just for supplies. Trash goes out by mule, and so does mail. Occasionally a very heavy piece of equipment will be helicoptered in.

Q. What is the unusual postmark from Phantom Ranch?
A. At Phantom Ranch you can buy postcards that are postmarked "Mailed by mule at the bottom of the Grand Canyon."

Q. Where do the Grand Canyon mules come from?
A. They are carefully selected from the best mule ranches in America. Grand Canyon mules are the NFL of the mule world, the super athletes. But they are also selected for their gentle, patient personalities.

Q. Why does the Grand Canyon use mules and not horses?
A. Mules have a better view of their feet than horses do—and

About 8,000 people ride mules from the South Rim every year.

thus can better see where they are placing their feet on the edge of a cliff. Mules also give a smoother ride, and they can do more work.

Q. How many years do Grand Canyon mules work on the trails?
   A) 5 to 10   B) 15 to 20   C) 25 to 30
A. B) 15 to 20.

Q. How many days a week do mules work?
A. It depends on the age of the mule. A young mule may work five days a week, but aging mules may work every other day and carry lighter riders.

> Joke: If a mule rider is nervous because it's the first time they've ever ridden a mule, wranglers tell them their mule is a perfect match for them, because it's the first time their mule has ever been ridden.

Q. How many Grand Canyon mules have fallen off the trail and killed riders?
   A) 12   B) 3   C) Zero
A. C) Zero. The scariest thing about riding a Grand Canyon mule is that they like to walk right on the edge of cliffs. But they have a perfect safety record.

> Joke: If mule riders ask wranglers what to do if they start to fall off, the wranglers tell them to be sure to keep their eyes open, since the scenery is so pretty on the fall to the bottom of the canyon.

Q. What's the record for the most miles ridden by a Grand Canyon mule wrangler?
A) 10,000 (16,009 km)   B) 25,000 (40,225 km)   C) 40,000 (64,360 km)
A. C) 40,000 (64,360 km), by Ross Knox, who is also a cowboy poet. That's more than 4,000 trips in and out of the canyon. One mule saddle has gone 54,000 miles (87,000 km) in the canyon.

Q. How long do mule shoes last on Grand Canyon trails?
   A) 3 weeks   B) 3 months   C) 1 year

The Grand Canyon has the oldest working blacksmith shop in America.

A. A) 3 weeks. Since some of the trail is on granite and schist, both hard rocks, the heavier mules can wear out their shoes in only three weeks.

Q. True or false: In the wintertime regular mule shoes are exchanged for "snow tires."
A. True. After a big snow, the trails can be snow packed and icy for weeks. For better traction the mules wear shoes with metal cleats.

Q. There's a 200-pound (91 kg) weight limit for riders on mules, but there's a famous photograph of a man riding a Grand Canyon mule, and he sure looks like he weighs more than 200 pounds. Who was he?
A. President Teddy Roosevelt. No one was bold enough to tell the president—a former Rough Rider—that he was too big to ride a mule. But when Teddy Roosevelt's successor, President William Howard Taft, visited the Grand Canyon in 1909, he had to ride a buggy. Taft weighed 350 pounds (159 kg).

Q. What did President Taft say when he first saw the Grand Canyon?
A. Taft said, "Golly, what a gully!"

Q. What was the strangest thing ever carried into the Grand Canyon by mule?
A. A piano was disassembled and carried down to Phantom Ranch. Long worn out, the piano is now buried in a filled-in swimming hole. In 1923 the Havasupai Indians used seven horses to carry the pieces of a grand piano to their village of Supai.

Blind people, 100-year-old people, and people with artificial legs have hiked the canyon.

During Prohibition, bootleggers hid a still down the Tanner Trail.

WILDLIFE

Q. How many species of mammals live at the Grand Canyon?
  A) 51   B) 91   C) 151
A. B) 91. They range from elk, which can be ten feet (3 m) long, to shrews, only three inches (7 cm) long.

Q. The largest animal in Grand Canyon National Park is the elk. Elk can weigh up to:
  A) 500 pounds (227 kg)   B) 750 pounds (340 kg)
                  C) 1,000 pounds (454 kg)
A. B) 750 pounds (340 kg). Elk in the Grand Canyon region are Rocky Mountain elk. They were transplanted here early in the 20th century to replace the native Merriam elk, which had been hunted to extinction.

Q. How much can elk antlers weigh?
  A) 30 pounds (13.6 kg)   B) 50 pounds (23 kg)
                  C) 75 pounds (34 kg)
A. B) Up to 50 pounds (23 kg). Male elk shed their antlers every spring and grow new ones at a rate of about half an inch (1.3 cm) per day.

Q. How much do desert bighorn sheep weigh?
  A) 150 pounds (68 kg)   B) 200 pounds (91 kg)
                  C) 250 pounds (114 kg)
A. C) 250 pounds (114 kg).

Q. How much do their horns weigh?
A. The curving horns of a large mature ram may weigh 30 pounds (13.6 kg).

Q. Where are you least likely to see bighorn sheep?
  A) Inside the canyon   B) Along the rim   C) In the forest
A. C) In the forest. Bighorn sheep rely on their agility on cliffs to avoid predators. You may see them on the canyon

rim, but they don't like to get far away from the steep edge of the rim.

Q. In the springtime bighorn sheep live high up in the canyon, and in the summer they live near the river. Why is this?
A. Bighorn sheep will stay at higher elevations where there is better forage as long as they can find water in springs and pot-holes. When this water dries up, they are forced to descend to the river and side streams.

Q. How many mountain lions inhabit the Grand Canyon?
   A) 500   B) 30   C) 12
A. Only the mountain lions know for sure. A century ago there were hundreds, but they were hunted to very small numbers. Today mountain lions live mainly in remote areas so no one is sure how many there are. One study showed that there are at least 12. The best guess is about 30. In the 1990s a mountain lion moved into Grand Canyon Village and started eating the pets of campers and residents.

Q. There is a wild cat that is more abundant than mountain lions at the Grand Canyon but rarely seen. What is it?
A. The bobcat. Bobcats are common but seldom seen because they are nocturnal.

Q. Do bears live at the Grand Canyon?
A. Not on a regular basis. There used to be grizzly bears on the North Rim. Occasionally a black bear wanders to the rim from the mountains near Flagstaff or the forests north of the North Rim. But bears need to eat lots of vegetation, like berries, so the Grand Canyon's arid environment isn't the best place for them.

Q. Were there ever any buffalo around the Grand Canyon?
A. Yes, but the arid Southwest didn't have the grasslands to support enormous herds of buffalo like those found on the Great Plains. Instead, there were small, scattered populations. In 1906 a man named Buffalo Jones set up a buffalo ranch near the Grand Canyon and attempted to crossbreed buffalo and cows

---

Jackrabbits can run 40 miles (64 km) per hour and leap 20 feet (6 m).

into "cattalo." It didn't work, but the buffalo ranch is still there. It was Buffalo Jones, while lecturing back east, who inspired writer Zane Grey to head west.

Q. True or false: Gray foxes climb juniper trees to eat the berries.
A. True. The gray fox is the only member of the dog family that climbs trees.

Q. The trunks of the trees at Phantom Ranch are wrapped in wire fencing. Why?
A. To stop beavers from cutting them down. Beavers in the Grand Canyon live in burrows along the river. They only dream of damming up the Colorado River.

Q. Does the Grand Canyon have coyotes and wolves?
A. Coyotes live throughout the canyon, from the river to the rim, with more on the rim. There used to be wolves but they were killed off by hunters, trappers, and settlers in the early 1900s.

Q. Mule deer are the most frequently seen large mammal at the Grand Canyon. They live both on the rim and in the inner canyon. They are called mule deer because their large ears are like mule ears, moving independently of one another. How much do mule deer weigh?
  A) 150 pounds (68 kg)   B) 250 pounds (113 kg)
                    C) 400 pounds (181 kg)
A. B) 250 pounds (113 kg). Mule deer are closely related to white-tailed deer but are found only in the western U. S., especially in the Southwest.

One of the textbook cases of ecological imbalance happened on the North Rim of the Grand Canyon. In the early 1900s hunters killed off most of the predators on the North Rim. "Uncle Jim" Owens, the North Rim game warden, personally killed 532 mountain lions and far more wolves and coyotes. Without predators, the deer population exploded, rising from a few thousand to an estimated 100,000 by 1924. The deer outgrew their food supply and stripped the forests bare. One winter tens of thousands of deer starved to death. The population crashed back to around 10,000.

The Grand Canyon has a family of albino bighorn sheep.

When the North Rim deer population exploded in 1924, a former horse thief proposed rounding up thousands of deer and driving them like cattle into the canyon, swimming them across the Colorado River, and herding them up to the South Rim. This plan won the support of Arizona's governor and got national attention. Western novelist Zane Grey and movie director D. W. Griffith came to record the deer drive. More than a hundred Navajos and cowboys lined up and beat on pots and pans to scare up the deer. But deer don't herd like cattle. They leaped past the herders and fled deeper into the forest. The deer drive was a total fiasco.

Q. How many burros live in the Grand Canyon?
  A) Hundreds   B) Dozens   C) Almost zero
A. C) Almost zero. Early prospectors used burros in the Grand Canyon and sometimes abandoned them there. The burro population increased into the hundreds and began out-competing native wildlife like desert bighorn sheep. Around 1980 wildlife experts removed 580 burros, even using helicopters to airlift them out of the canyon. Today a few burros probably wander into the western canyon from the lands above, and river guides occasionally report hearing burros braying, but no one is sure how many there are.

Q. Pack rats are foot-long (1/3 m) rodents that build huge nests out of twigs, bones, and anything else they can find, and then they cement the nest together with urine. How many years can a pack rat nest last?
  A) Dozens of years B) Hundreds   C) Thousands
A. C) Thousands of years if it's in a sheltered spot. This longevity makes pack rat nests valuable to biologists, who study the nests to find out what kind of vegetation and food was present long ago.

During the Ice Age, giant ground sloths lived in Grand Canyon caves. One cave was so heavily used that it built up large deposits of sloth dung. In the 1920s park ranger Eddie McKee climbed to a cave outside the park and brought

---

One radio-collared mountain lion crossed from rim to rim...

> home some sloth dung to add to his natural history collection. Eddie's wife Barbara was a biologist, but there were limits to her love of nature. When Eddie displayed the sloth dung atop their piano, Barbara insisted it had to go.

Q. Was a "Lost World" with dinosaurs discovered in the Grand Canyon?
A. No, but in 1937 headlines across America announced that the American Museum of Natural History was sending an expedition to the Grand Canyon to search for dinosaurs in a lost worldon Shiva Temple, an isolated and inaccessible mesa. In truth, the museum was looking for much smaller species, such as insects. It turned out that Shiva Temple wasn't so isolated or inaccessible after all, and there was nothing special about its inhabitants.

Q. What's the most dangerous animal at the Grand Canyon?
  A) Mountain Lions   B) Rattlesnakes   C) Squirrels
A. C) The rock squirrel. Even though it is illegal to feed any animal in the park, some tourists still try to feed rock squirrels and often get bitten by mistake. Rock squirrels can carry rabies and plague, so bite victims require medical care.

Q. True or false: Grand Canyon deer once became addicted to cigarettes.
A. True. Back in the 1930s tourists weren't satisfied with giving food to the deer, they also started feeding them cigarettes. Park residents believed that the deer became addicted to nicotine and began aggressively seeking cigarettes.

Q. In addition to being illegal, giving human food to wildlife harms the wildlife. Why?
A. Our food, especially junk food, contains too much salt. In a dry environment animals can't find enough water to balance this salt, and they become ill, even losing their fur. There are other problems too. For example, deer who seek food in campgrounds will eat sandwiches still wrapped in plastic. The plastic accumulates inside their intestines and prevents them from digesting food.

...including swimming the Colorado River, in only 8 hours!

Q. Each rim of the Grand Canyon has a distinct subspecies of tree squirrel. The North Rim has the Kaibab squirrel, the South Rim the Abert squirrel. Kaibab squirrels have a black belly and a white tail, and Abert squirrels have a white belly and a gray tail. Biologists think that 10,000 years ago the two squirrels belonged to the same species. What turned them into separate subspecies?
A. During the last Ice Age some 10,000 years ago, forests stretched far down into the Grand Canyon, and the squirrels from each rim could migrate and interbreed. As the climate dried up and the forests retreated to the rims, the squirrels on each rim were left isolated.

Q. Why does the Kaibab squirrel have a white tail?
A. The Kaibab squirrel had to adapt to the heavier winters on the North Rim and evolved a white tail to blend in with snow.

Q. True or False: Just as the Wild West was troubled by horse and cattle rustlers, the Grand Canyon has been hit by butterfly rustlers.
A. True. The North Rim hosts a rare butterfly called the Kaibab swallowtail. Poachers have stolen specimens and sold them on the butterfly black market for $400 each.

Q. How many species of reptiles live at the Grand Canyon?
   A) 25   B) 50   C) 500
A. B) About 50 lizards and snakes, and a desert tortoise.

Q. The zebra-tailed lizard runs by lifting its front feet off the ground and running on its hind legs only. How fast can it run this way, in miles per hour?
   A) 2 miles (3 km)   B) 5 (8 km)   C) 18 (29 km)
A. C) It has been clocked at 18 miles (29 km) per hour.

Q. What does the southern desert horned lizard do with its blood to defend itself from predators?
A. It squirts blood from its eyes. It can squirt blood up to 6 feet (2 m).

Wild turkeys live on both rims.

Q. What does the northern plateau lizard do with its tail to defend itself from predators?
A. Sheds it. The tail continues to wiggle, distracting predators while the lizard escapes. The tail regenerates, but in some studies 40 percent of lizards lacked tails.

Q. Of Grand Canyon lizards, what's unusual about the chuckwalla?
   A) Doesn't drink; gets all its water from its food.
   B) Vegetarian; it ignores bugs for leaves.
   C) It flushes salt through its nose, not through its urine like other animals.
   D) All of the above
A. D) All of the above. Not only that, the chuckwalla remains active in heat that keeps other lizards hiding in the shade.

Q. Are there Gila monsters in the Grand Canyon?
A. Yes, but only in the western end of the canyon. Gila monsters are America's largest lizard and the only poisonous one. They stay underground all day and are rarely seen by humans.

Q. What's the most poisonous creature in the Grand Canyon?
   A) Rattlesnakes   B) Scorpions   C) Red ants
A. C) Red ants. On an ounce-by-ounce basis, the venom of the harvester ant (usually called the red ant) is more potent than the venom of rattlesnakes or scorpions. Of course, the bite of a red ant delivers a much smaller dosage of poison than a rattlesnake bite or scorpion sting. Still, red ant bites can be intensely painful. Grand Canyon river runners are careful not to drop food scraps in camping areas because a steady supply of food will attract a steady supply of ants. It's easy to accidentally pinch an ant with a finger or toe, and the ants pinch back!

Q. Which is the least dangerous?
   A) TarantulasB) Scorpions   C) Rattlesnakes
A. A) Tarantulas. Their venom is very mild, hurting less than a bee sting, and they rarely bite people. Their fearsome reputation is owed mainly to their size and to too many Hollywood movies.

Grey foxes will eat the fruit of prickly pear cactus.

Q. What gruesome fate awaits tarantulas that are attacked by a certain wasp?

A. At the Grand Canyon, tarantulas are prey for a large wasp called the tarantula wasp, which stings and paralyzes the tarantula, lays its egg on it, then buries it alive. The tarantula serves as food for the wasp larva.

Q. The bark scorpion is the most common scorpion found in the Grand Canyon. It also has the deadliest poison of the 90 scorpions in North America. How many humans are known to have died from scorpion stings in the Grand Canyon?

A) 100   B) 25   C) Zero

A. C) Zero. But it's not from lack of trying. Rangers estimate that of every 200 people who camp inside the canyon, one gets stung by a scorpion. Most of these stings could be avoided through simple precautions such as shaking out boots and clothes before putting them on. But scorpion venom was designed for killing scorpion-sized prey, not large mammals. The last recorded scorpion-caused death in Arizona was in 1964. If you are on the rim there's little worry it's too cool for scorpions.

Q. How many people are known to have died from rattlesnake bites in the Grand Canyon?

A) Zero   B) 20   C) 50

A. A) Zero. Cowboy movies, which usually feature western diamondback rattlesnakes, have portrayed rattlesnakes as aggressive critters. The Grand Canyon does have diamondbacks, but another species, the Grand Canyon rattlesnake, is quite mellow. You can walk right past it and it may not even bother to rattle. Most of the rattlesnake bites in the canyon happen when people, usually young males, try to prove how brave they are by catching a rattlesnake; the snakes are not amused.

> It was ranger-naturalist Eddie McKee who in 1929 first recognized that the Grand Canyon held a unique species of rattlesnake. McKee was hiking in the canyon when he spotted an unusual pink-colored rattlesnake. Since he lacked any container to put it in, he grabbed the snake behind its head and carried it out of the canyon. Reaching his car, he still couldn't find any container, so he held the

Navajos call the coyote "God's dog."

rattlesnake out the window with one hand and drove home with his other hand.

Q. Why is the Grand Canyon rattlesnake colored pink?
A. To blend in with the reddish canyon rocks.

Q. How many species of amphibians live in the Grand Canyon?
A) 7   B) 70   C) 700
A. A) 7. Due to the lack of water in most of the canyon, there's only 7 species of toads, frogs, and salamanders.

Q. How many species of birds are found at the Grand Canyon?
A) 150   B) 250   C) 370
A. C) More than 370 species have been spotted, but many of these are just migrating through. A bit less than half of these species nest at the canyon, and a bit more than 10 percent live at the canyon year-round.

Q. Glen Canyon Dam harmed the native fish in the Grand Canyon, but it benefited birds. Why is this?
A. Before Glen Canyon Dam, annual spring floods ripped out all the vegetation along the river. Now there is a stable zone of trees and bushes along the river, which makes great bird habitat. About 75 percent of Grand Canyon birds depend on this riparian zone.

Q. Why did bald eagles begin wintering in the Grand Canyon after Glen Canyon Dam was built?
A. Before the dam, the Colorado River was too silty for eagles to spot fish, but now the water is usually clear. Also, the cold-water river now has trout, which spawn in shallow side creeks where they are easy targets.

Q. In addition to bald eagles, what other birds of prey live at the Grand Canyon?
A. There are golden eagles and more than a dozen species of hawks, falcons, and owls.

Q. The Grand Canyon has America's largest population of what falcon?

Snakes have no ears. They "hear" vibrations in the ground.

A. Peregrine falcons. Peregrine falcons, once an endangered species, find Grand Canyon cliffs to be perfect habitat.

Q. One of the most common birds at the Grand Canyon is the raven. What's the difference between ravens and crows?
A. Ravens are larger, as large as hawks, and have a heavier beak. Ravens can thrive in wilderness areas from the arctic to deserts, while crows are more common in agricultural areas, which is why you see scarecrows and not scareravens. At the Grand Canyon, ravens are agile and playful flyers.

Q. True or false: Ravens are so smart that they can watch a hiker put food into a backpack pocket, wait until the hiker is away, fly to the backpack, unzip the pocket, and remove the food.
A. True. Scientific studies of raven intelligence have shown them to be amazingly smart birds. In the Grand Canyon they are adept at stealing unattended food from campgrounds and river rafts, and they have learned how to go trout fishing by watching eagles catch trout in the river's side streams.

Q. If you are standing on the rim in summer and hear swishing sounds and see birds diving into the canyon, what are they?
A. Probably swifts and swallows, which dive swiftly in pursuit of flying insects. Both have dark wings and white bellies, but the white-throated swift's wings are longer and more pointed, while the violet-green swallow has a green back. As fast as swifts and swallows are, peregrine falcons can catch them in flight.

Q. Hummingbirds at the Grand Canyon may winter in Mexico and migrate north. How fast can they fly, in miles per hour?
  A) 10 (16 km)   B) 20 (32 km)   C) 30 (48 km)
A. C) 30 miles per hour (48 km). To do so they may beat their wings up to 80 times per second.

Q. True or false: The Grand Canyon once held vampires.
A. True. Vampire bats, that is. Excavations in caves have revealed that during the last Ice Age vampire bats lived in the canyon, sucking the blood of large Ice Age mammals.

Snakes can eat up to 50 percent of their body weigh in one meal.

Q. By the 1980s, how many California condors were left in the whole world?

   A) 22   B) 222   C) 2,222

A. A) Only 22. Biologists feared that the condors would soon be extinct. In 1987 the remaining condors were removed from the wild for a captive breeding program. Within five years their population had climbed to 63, and some condors were released to the wild in California. In 1996, six condors were released at the Vermillion Cliffs just north of the Grand Canyon. By 2013 the total condor population in the wild was about 240, with about 80 in the Grand Canyon region.

Q. After California condors were released at the Vermillion Cliffs, how many years did it take for them to start nesting and laying eggs inside the Grand Canyon?

   A) 1 year   B) 5 years   C) 10 years

A. B) 5 years. The first condor eggs were laid in 2001 but failed to hatch. The next year, condors settled in caves near Grand Canyon Village. Two pairs produced eggs, but again the eggs failed to hatch, a common occurrence for condors. Finally in 2003 a condor chick hatched in the Grand Canyon.

Q. The California condor has many similarities with another Grand Canyon bird, the turkey vulture. How do you tell them apart?

A. The condor is twice as large, about 4-feet (1.2 m) tall at rest compared with about 2-feet (0.6 m) tall for turkey vultures, but the canyon's scale can make a 2-foot difference difficult to recognize. The turkey vulture has white on the trailing edge of its wings; the condor has white on the leading edge. The turkey vulture flies with its wings canted upward to form a "V" shape and often pivots from side to side; the condor keeps its wings spread flat.

Q. On their wings, condors have tags with numbers, and radio transmitters. Why?

A. The condors are closely monitored by biologists. The numbers and radio transmitters allow biologists to track the movements and activities of every bird. Each transmitter has a unique frequency for telling birds apart.

Red-spotted toads absorb moisture from damp rocks.

Q. What's the wingspan of a California condor?
   A) 6 feet (1.8 m)   B) 9.5 feet (2.9 m)
                C) 15 feet (4.5 m)
A. B) 9.5 feet (2.9 m). By contrast, the American bald eagle's wingspan is 8 feet (2.4 m).

Q. How much does a condor weigh?
   A) 15 pounds (7 kg)   B) 22 pounds (10 kg)   C) 40 pounds (18 kg)
A. B) Up to 22 pounds (10 kg).

Q. What do condors eat?
A. Carrion dead animals. Their beaks and talons aren't designed for hunting; they have to find food that is already dead. But their beaks are strong enough to snap small bones. Condors prefer large animals like deer but will settle for squirrels.

Q. How do condors find their food?
   A) Smell   B) Sight   C) Watching other animals
A. C) They watch other animals, especially scavengers like ravens, vultures, and coyotes.

Q. As many as 30 condors have been seen hanging around Grand Canyon Village in the spring and summer. Are they waiting for something to die?
A. Yes you! In the Ice Age, condors survived by following herds of large mammals and waiting for some of the animals to die. Today the largest herds of animals are the tourists on the South Rim. This makes Grand Canyon Village the best spot in the world for observing condors. In the winter you aren't likely to see condors because the warm updrafts they rely on for soaring aren't present, and the condors move to warmer deserts.

Q. Why are condor heads bare of feathers?
A. As carrion eaters, condors stick their heads into dead bodies. Feathers would get messy with flesh, blood, and bugs. After eating, condors often go to water to wash off.

Q. How long can condors live?
   A) 25 years   B) 50 years   C) 60 years
A. C) 60 years.

_____

The smallest bat at the canyon, the western pipistrelle...

Q. Because carrion can be hard to find, condors have to eat as much as possible when they can. To help, they have an expandable pouch, or crop, inside their throat. How much meat can a crop hold?
 A) 1 pound (0.5 kg)   B) 2 pounds (0.9 kg)   C) 3 pounds (1.4 kg)
A. C) 3 pounds (1.4 kg). This is about 15 percent of a condor's weight.

Q. How long can condors go without eating?
 A) Two days   B) One week   C) Two weeks
A. C) Two weeks.

Q. Condors lay one egg about 5 inches (12 cm) long. Condors incubate eggs for two months. Once it starts, how long does it take for a condor chick to break out of its egg?
 A) 3 hours   B) 1 day   C) 3 days
A. C) Almost 3 days.

Q. How long does it take for baby condors to fly for the first time and leave the nest?
 A) 3 months   B) 6 months   C) 12 months
A. B) 6 months.

Q. How far can condors fly in a day?
 A) 10 miles (16 km)   B) 50 miles (80 km)   C) 100 miles (160 km)
A. C) 100 miles (160 km).

Q. How high can condors fly?
 A) 1 mile (1.6 km)   B) 2 miles (3.2 km)   C) 3 miles (4.8 km)
A. C) 3 miles (4.8 km).

Q. Some Grand Canyon caves hold the bones of an Ice Age bird even larger than California condors. It was called the teratorn, or "monster bird." It stood 4 feet tall and weighed 50 pounds. How long was its wingspan?
 A) 10 feet (3 m)   B) 12 feet (3.6 m)   C) 20 feet (6 m)
A. B) 12 feet (3.6 m). By contrast, a condor has a 9.5-foot (2.9 m) wingspan.

... is one of few bats to bear twins.

Q. True or False: Condors urinate on their legs to stay cool.
A. True. Being a big black bird in a desert can make you hot. By urinating on their legs, condors use evaporative cooling. This also stains their legs white.

Q. What's the greatest threat to condors?
   A) Coyotes   B) Humans   C) Eagles
A. Humans. Condors will eat human trash, such as plastic bags, and even feed it to their chicks, killing the chicks. Condors have died from lead poisoning after eating lead bullets inside dead game. They've also gotten lead poisoning by swallowing coins that tourists toss off the rim. Poachers have deliberately shot condors. The first condor shooting happened inside Grand Canyon National Park in 1997, only a year after they were released. Hunting is prohibited in national parks.

When bighorn sheep knock horns, the sound can echo for miles in the canyon.

The European starling, introduced in New York in 1890, reached Grand Canyon by 1955.

The canyon wren makes the canyon's most famous birdcall, a descending trill.

Today's condors are nesting in the same caves used by Ice Age condors.

A condor skull 12,000 years old was found in a Grand Canyon cave.

Native Americans

Q. How old is the oldest human-made artifact found at the Grand Canyon?
　　A) 1,000 years old　　B) 5,000 years　　　　C) 12,000 years
A. C) 12,000 years old. It was part of a Clovis point used for hunting at the end of the Ice Age. It was discovered on the South Rim in 2005 by a bird watcher wandering in the woods.

Q. For more than 10,000 years the humans who lived in and around the Grand Canyon were hunter-gatherers. Since they moved around in search of game, they didn't build houses or leave many traces of their presence. But they did leave some animal-shaped figurines made out of willow twigs. These figurines have been dated to 2,500-4,000 years old. Some figurines look like deer and have spear-like twigs sticking through them, which suggests they were used in hunting magic. Where were these figurines found?
　　A) Inside pottery　　B) Buried in the ground　　C) In caves
A. C) In caves. Some of these caves are difficult to reach, and show no signs of human habitation, which suggests they were used strictly for ceremonial purposes.

Q. As time passed, Native Americans made their projectile points smaller and smaller. Why?
　　A) As Ice Age animals died out, game was smaller.
　　B) The invention of the bow and arrow made smaller points just as effective.
　　C) Both of the above
A. C) Both of the above.

Q. Most Native American projectile points are made from chert (often called flint), a mineral nodule found in limestone. But the best points are made from obsidian, a black, glassy material. Where does obsidian come from?
　　A) Volcanoes　　　　B) Meteorites　　　　　C) Geysers

A. A) Volcanoes. Each volcano has a unique chemical fingerprint, so archaeologists can tell which volcano a piece of obsidian came from. Most of the obsidian in the Grand Canyon area came from one volcano, now called Government Mountain, near Williams, Arizona. The obsidian from this volcano was so excellent that Native Americans traded it over hundred of miles.

Q. After 10,000 years of a hunter-gatherer culture, human inhabitants of the Grand Canyon became farmers. What brought about this change of lifestyle from hunting to farming?
A. The spread of corn from Mexico, where it had been grown for thousands of years. Along with corn came beans and squash. Corn, beans, and squash could grow in a desert environment, provided balanced nutrition, and offered good crop rotation so that the soil wouldn't be depleted.

Q. Who were these Grand Canyon farmers?
A. These were the Ancestral Puebloans, also called Anasazi. They were the ancestors of today's Pueblo tribes. They lived in the canyon about 1,000 years ago.

Q. True or false: When Native Americans became farmers, they gave up hunting.
A. False. In one respect, hunting became even easier. When you grow crops in a desert, you are sure to attract lots of rabbits and deer. Farmers had to be good hunters just to defend their crops. The Ancestral Puebloans built ingenious snares to catch rabbits, and used bows and arrows to have an occasional feast of deer.

Q. True or false: The Ancestral Puebloans ate cactus.
A. True. Native Americans knew every use of nature, especially in a desert where resources are limited. Ancestral Puebloans gathered edible cactus, especially prickly pear cactus.

Q. True or false: The Ancestral Puebloans ate agave.
A. True. They roasted agave, which isn't a cactus, but anyone who fell onto agave's sharp bayonets wouldn't be comforted by

---

Some ancient pottery bears the fingerprints of its makers.

this distinction. Native Americans used the same agave roasting pits for decades, even centuries, building up piles of rock dozens of feet across.

Q. What is particularly unusual about one species of agave at the Grand Canyon?
A. One species of agave at the Grand Canyon is found only around archaeology sites; it seems to have been obtained through trading from Mexico as a cultivated food crop.

Q. Is there any Native American rock art in the Grand Canyon?
A. Quite a bit, but since it's usually hidden under cliffs, it's hard to find. The Ancestral Puebloans often painted and pecked images like bighorn sheep, snakes, and rain clouds. The hunter-gatherers who lived in the Grand Canyon thousands of years ago painted elaborate shamanistic murals.

Q. Which is older: Egyptian hieroglyphs or Grand Canyon rock art?
A. The oldest hieroglyphs are more than 5,000 years old. The oldest Grand Canyon rock art is thought to be about 4,000 years old.

Q. How many Native American archaeological sites have been found in Grand Canyon National Park?
    A) 500   B) 1,000   C) 4,000
A. C) More than 4,000 sites are known, but there are undoubtedly many thousands more. Only 5 percent of the area of Grand Canyon National Park has been systematically surveyed for archaeological sites. Most sites were created by the Ancestral Puebloans, especially between the years 1050 and 1150 AD. These sites consist of houses, kivas, farming terraces, check dams, garden borders, granaries, rock art, roasting pits, pot sherds, projectile points, and piles of chert discarded in the making of projectile points. Most settlements were small, only a few houses for a few families.

Q. Where can a park visitor see a Native American archaeological site?
A. Two ruins are open for visitors: Tusayan Ruin and Museum on the South Rim near Desert View, and Walhalla Glades on the North Rim.

Pottery was a high-tech invention, replacing woven baskets.

Q. How can archaeologists establish the age of ruins?
A. Early in the 20ᵗʰ century Andrew Douglass, an Arizona astronomer, realized that the wood used in Ancestral Puebloan buildings provided a tree ring map of the past. By matching the patterns of thicker and thinner tree rings from log to log he built a time chart that goes back more than two thousand years. By matching up tree rings, you can tell exactly what year a tree in a ruin was cut. Another method involves pottery. Pottery designs changed frequently, so when you find a particular pottery design in a ruin, this could date a ruin to within a 25-year period. Radiocarbon dating can date organic matter, but has a large margin of error.

> Joke: One time a tourist visiting a Grand Canyon ruin asked a ranger: "Why did the Indians always live in ruins?"

Q. The Grand Canyon was far from the centers of Ancestral Puebloan society, such as Chaco Canyon and Mesa Verde, but trade goods found at the Grand Canyon prove that canyon residents were in contact with distant places. What are these trade goods?
   A) Pottery from the Four Corners area
   B) Tropical bird feathers from Mexico
   C) Shell beads from the Pacific coast
   D) All of the above
A. D) All of the above.

Q. The Ancestral Puebloans built stone walls high up on cliffs to create rooms that were too small to live in. What were they for?
A. For storing grain. Deer couldn't climb cliffs, and the Puebloans sealed up the entrances with slabs and mud to keep out mice and bugs.

Q. Walking in a rocky canyon requires sturdy footwear. What did the Ancestral Puebloans use to make sandals?
A. Yucca, a cactus-like plant that contains thick, tough fibers. The Puebloans also wove these fibers into ropes.

Q. For clothes Native Americans often wore animal hides or hairs. But the Ancestral Puebloans in the Grand Canyon also grew a crop to use for clothing. What was it?
A. Cotton.

John Wesley Powell was fascinated by Native Americans...

Q. True or false: Native Americans used the stringy bark of juniper trees as diapers.
A. True. The soft fibers can absorb lots of moisture.

Q. Did the Ancestral Puebloans live inside the Grand Canyon all year?
A. Some did, but many migrated up to the rim in the spring to grow crops on soil watered by snowmelt. The rim was also much cooler in the summer. By the time snow began falling on the rim, they returned into the canyon to spend the winter.

Q. Why did the Ancestral Puebloans finally leave the Grand Canyon?
A. A long drought made it impossible for them to continue farming. They headed for areas that offered reliable springs, such as the Hopi mesas.

Q. By what year did the Ancestral Puebloans abandon the Grand Canyon?
    A) 1000 AD   B) 1225   C) 1500
A. B) Around 1225. One of the last villages built at the Grand Canyon was Tusayan on the South Rim, built around 1185. Within 40 years it was abandoned. Today Tusayan Ruin holds a museum about Native American life at the Grand Canyon.

Q. The Hopis are a tribe that lives in northeastern Arizona, about 50 miles (80 km) from the Grand Canyon. They are descended from the Ancestral Puebloans who lived in the Grand Canyon a thousand years ago. Do the Hopis and the Ancestral Puebloans have many similarities?
A. Yes. Both are desert farmers, even growing the same crops, like corn. Both build pueblos, or stone buildings. The Hopis build kivas, or underground ceremonial chambers, with many of the same symbolic features you can see in the kiva at Tusayan Ruin. In Hopi creation stories, their place of emergence is a spring at the bottom of the Grand Canyon. For centuries the Hopis made a pilgrimage to gather salt from the bottom of the canyon.

Q. There are kivas on the South Rim and inside the canyon, but none on the North Rim. What does this pattern mean?

. . .and founded the American Bureau of Ethnology to study their cultures.

A. The North Rim was inhabited only during the summer. Today, the kachina ceremonies of the Hopis take place most of the year but not during the summer, so in the summer kivas are not so essential. The lack of kivas on the North Rim suggests that the Ancestral Puebloans practiced a ceremonial cycle similar to the Hopis.

The Navajos, whose lands border the eastern Grand Canyon, have the largest reservation and the second largest population of any tribe in America. Their success is especially remarkable considering that they arrived in the Four Corners region relatively recently, not long before the Spanish. They succeeded because much of the Southwest had been abandoned by the Puebloans due to drought, and the Navajos grazed livestock, the only lifestyle that could succeed in the Four Corners region.

The same drought that drove the Ancestral Puebloans out of the Grand Canyon (and brought down Puebloan centers like Chaco Canyon) also forced desert tribes out of the Mohave Desert and the Great Basin and into higher terrain where water, vegetation, and game were more available. This is how the Paiutes, Hualapai, and Havasupai came to live at the Grand Canyon. They continued their hunter-gatherer lifestyle, but in Havasu Canyon, a side canyon of the Grand Canyon, the Havasupai found one of the few places where a farming lifestyle was still possible.

Q. How many Havasupai live inside the Grand Canyon?
    A) 200   B) 500   C) 1,000
A. B) About 500. They live in a village called Supai, located in a side canyon called Havasu canyon, which is famous for its waterfalls and travertine pools. Supai has a school, medical clinic, and churches, but no cars because there's no road from the rim. The Havasupai rely on horses.

Q. The Havasupai and Hualapai both have "pai" in their name, and they are neighboring tribes. Are they related?
A. Yes, closely. The Hualapais had been hunters and gatherers, but about 500 years ago a few Hualapai families moved into

---

Navajos traditionally believed that the Grand Canyon was...

Havasu Canyon and adopted a new lifestyle—farming. The word "pai" means "people," and the word "Hualapai" means "people of the tall pines." The Hualapais who settled in Havasu Canyon renamed themselves the Havasupai, which means "people of the blue-green water."

Q. The Havasupais hold a festival every year that features one of the crops they grow. What is it?
    A) Peaches   B) Corn   C) Squash
A. A) Peaches. The Peach Festival draws visitors, including many members of other tribes, from hundreds of miles away.

Q. How many tourists visit Havasu Canyon every year?
    A) 10,000   B) 20,000   C) 30,000
A. C) About 30,000. Most visitors hike in on an 8-mile (12 km) trail; about 25 percent of visitors ride in on horses; and a few use a helicopter.

Q. Supai, the Havasupai village, is the only village in America where mail is still delivered by horse and mule. When did this mail delivery begin?
    A) 1893   B) 1932   C) 1945
A. A) 1893.

> Traditionally the Havasupai farmed inside their canyon from spring until fall and then moved onto the plateau above to hunt and gather in the winter. But in 1882 the U.S. government confined the Havasupai to a tiny reservation that included only their village and fields, disrupting their traditional migration. It took nearly a century for the Havasupai to get Congress to return their plateau lands to tribal control.

Q. Is it possible to meet Native Americans at the Grand Canyon?
A. Some National Park Service employees are Native Americans, including interpreters who give programs about Native American history and culture. A dozen miles (20 km) east of Desert View is the Navajo reservation. At dozens of roadside stands, Navajos sell jewelry and other crafts, and visitors have a chance to talk with them about Navajo culture. For a large

---

...carved by the horn of a bighorn sheep.

selection of high-quality crafts and for a menu of Navajo foods, try the Cameron Trading Post 32 miles (51 km) east of Desert View. The Cameron Trading Post is one of the few historic Arizona trading posts still in operation.

Architect Mary Colter built two South Rim tributes to Native American culture. One is Hopi House, a 3-story Hopi pueblo. It opened in 1905 to serve as a gift shop for Native American arts and crafts. For many years Hopi families lived upstairs, performed dances for the public, and made crafts for sale. Today Hopi House still offers the best selection and quality of Native American art and crafts in the park. Colter's masterpiece is the Desert View Watchtower, whose interior contains murals depicting Hopi life and lore. The murals were painted by Hopi artist Fred Kaboti, and include a depiction of the legend of Tiyo, a Hopi youth who voyaged down the Colorado River in a hollow log, encountered the snake people, and brought the secret of rain to the Hopi people.

Q. In 1931 Albert Einstein visited the Grand Canyon. When he stopped at Hopi House he was crowned with a long Indian headdress with large feathers, and a photographer took a famous photo of Einstein in this headdress. What was wrong with this photo?

A. The Indian headdress had nothing to do with the Hopis or any Southwestern tribe. Long headdresses were worn by Great Plains tribes, who lived in teepees and hunted buffalo. Grand Canyon area tribes never lived in teepees: the Hopis lived in stone pueblos, the Navajos in wood and earthen hogans, and the Havasupai and Hualapai in brush wikiups.

At the Hopi villages, Hopis threw broken pottery over the edge of the mesa. For years the Hopis who lived at Hopi House would toss broken pottery from the shop over the rim of the canyon. In the 1930s the kids of white rangers began climbing over the edge, retrieving this broken pottery, and selling it to tourists as ancient Anasazi relics. When their ranger parents found out, they put a stop to it.

Navajos and Apaches are closely related tribes.

The Fred Harvey Company played a large role in making art and crafts a viable career for Native Americans. Until 1900 or so, most Native Americans made pottery or rugs for their own use or for trading at the trading post. Few white tourists ever got to the trading posts. When the Fred Harvey Company built its chain of shops across the Southwest, it connected affluent whites with Native American artisans and made it possible for Native Americans to make a living from their artwork from preserving and honoring their culture.

Pictographs are painted onto rocks, petroglyphs are pecked or scratched.

With its drumbeat similar to Native American music, reggae music has long been wildly popular among the Hopi and Havasupai.

The first white man to see Havasu Canyon was a Spanish missionary in 1776.

The Havasupai once farmed at Indian Garden, the oasis below Grand Canyon Village.

There are old Havasupai sweat lodges in the woods of the South Rim.

Havasu Creek drains 3,000 square miles (7,692 sq km, such a large drainage makes it prone to flash floods.

HISTORY

Q. The Spanish were the first Europeans to see the Grand Canyon. Which happened earlier: the Spanish discovery of the Grand Canyon or the pilgrims landing on Plymouth Rock?
A. The Spanish discovered the Grand Canyon in 1540, only 48 years after Columbus landed in the Americas. The pilgrims didn't arrive for another 80 years, in 1620. The Spanish discovery of the Grand Canyon also came 45 years before the Roanoke colony in Virginia in 1585, and 25 years before the Spanish settlement of St. Augustine, Florida, in 1565.

Q. True or false: When the Spanish discovered the Grand Canyon, Michelangelo was still painting the Sistine Chapel.
A. True.

Q. What were the Spanish searching for when they discovered the Grand Canyon?
   A) Gold   B) Furs   C) California
A. A) Gold. The Spanish had heard a legend that the Southwest held seven cities made of gold. The Coronado expedition went to find them but found only mud and stone pueblos. The Puebloans, perhaps eager to get rid of the Spanish, told them that the seven cities of gold lay farther west. Instead, the Spanish found the Grand Canyon.

Q. The Spanish who found the Grand Canyon tried to hike down to the river. Did they succeed?
A. No. They got only one-third of the way down. The scale of the canyon deceived them. When those who had hiked into the canyon returned to those who had stayed on the rim, they reported that what seemed to be mere rocks in the canyon were actually giant boulders taller than the tallest towers back in Spain.

Q. Which happened earlier: the Lewis and Clark Expedition or the first arrival of a United States citizen at the Grand Canyon?

When the Grand Canyon became a national park...

A. The Lewis and Clark Expedition. The first American citizen saw the Grand Canyon in 1826, nearly 300 years after the Spanish reached it.

Q. Who were the first United States citizens to see the Grand Canyon?
A. In 1826 some fur trappers were exploring northern Arizona and came upon the Grand Canyon. One of them, James Ohio Pattie, was disgusted that the canyon made it impossible to get to the beaver in the river. He called the canyon "horrid mountains that caged up the Colorado River and made it useless."

Q. Who was the first United States citizen to live at the Grand Canyon?
A. John Hance was a prospector who grew up in a mining area in the Missouri Ozarks. In 1883 he settled near Grandview Point on the South Rim, discovered a rich asbestos lode inside the canyon, and built a trail to it. When his first trail washed out, he tried a new route and built today's New Hance Trail. When the first tourists arrived on the South Rim they sought out John Hance for food and water and advice. Soon Hance realized that there was more money in the pockets of tourists than there was in mining. He became the first Grand Canyon tour guide, leading people down his trail and telling them tall tales. In 1919 he became the first person buried in the Grand Canyon park cemetery.

One day John Hance started telling a stranger what a great hunter he was, and that he had just shot a dozen deer. The stranger said: "Do you know who I am? I'm the game warden, and you've broken the law." John Hance replied: "Do you know who I am? I'm John Hance, and I'm the biggest damn liar in Arizona!"

Q. True or false: John Hance wore off the tip of his index finger by constantly pointing to the scenery for tourists.
A. True. At least, John Hance always claimed it was true.

...there were only 4 rangers.

Q. Where was the first hotel at the Grand Canyon?
A. At the bottom of the canyon. In 1884 J. H. Farlee built an 8-room hotel beside the Colorado River at the mouth of Diamond Creek, which is about 100 miles west of where John Hance had settled the year before. Getting to Farlee's hotel required a tortuous journey down a creek bed, and in the summer it was brutally hot. Farlee closed his hotel a few years later as the South Rim began attracting tourists.

For almost 20 years, the center of Grand Canyon tourism was the Grandview area. This is where John Hance lived, and where Pete Berry soon built the Grandview Trail to his mine on Horseshoe Mesa. Grandview became the destination of the stage coach from Flagstaff and the location of several camps or hotels. When the Santa Fe Railway arrived on the South Rim in 1901 and built Grand Canyon Village, the Grandview facilities couldn't compete. The 2-story log Grandview Hotel was later torn down, but you can still see its logs today: architect Mary Colter used them in the ceiling of the round entrance room of the Desert View Watchtower.

Q. Buckey O'Neill was an early prospector at the Grand Canyon. His cabin was incorporated into the Bright Angel Lodge and can be rented by guests today. Inside the canyon is O'Neill Butte. In addition to a love of the Grand Canyon, what did O'Neill have in common with Teddy Roosevelt?
A. Both became Rough Riders in the Spanish-American War and fought at the battle of San Juan Hill. But whereas Teddy Roosevelt became a national hero, O'Neill got killed.

Q. In the 1950s a mining company spent more than $3 million to reach a Grand Canyon cave full of bat guano or dung. Guano makes great fertilizer. The mining company estimated there was 100,000 tons of bat guano in the cave, worth about $15 million. But someone goofed. How much bat guano was really there?
    A) 1,000 tons   B) 10,000 tons   C) 25,000 tons
A. A) Only 1,000 tons. It was gone in about two weeks, and then the mine closed. The bats moved back in. Today the over-

---

The Grand Canyon's first museum was funded by The Brooklyn Eagle...

look across the river from this cave is called Guano Point; it's on Hualapai Indian lands, near their Skywalk.

Q. True or false: A railroad company planned to build a railroad down the entire inside length of the Grand Canyon.
A. True. In the Rocky Mountains it was often easiest to build railroads by following river corridors. In 1889 a Denver railroad company launched the Brown-Stanton river expedition to survey the Grand Canyon for a railroad.
The expedition was a disaster, drowning three men, Peter Hansbrough, Henry Richards, and the company president, Frank Brown. The railroad was never attempted.

Q. When the Santa Fe Railway reached the South Rim in 1901, how much did a ticket cost to reach the canyon from Williams, a town on the Santa Fe main line 60 miles away?
   A) $20   B) $10.50   C) $3.95
A. C) $3.95, or about $100 in today's dollars.

Q. E. P. Ripley was the Santa Fe Railway president who built the railway to the Grand Canyon. The name E. P. Ripley was later given to the steam locomotive at a famous theme park. Which theme park?
A. Disneyland. The railroad even runs through a "Grand Canyon."

Q. Today the Grand Canyon Railway stages a mock Wild West train robbery. Early in the 20th century there was no bank on the South Rim and trains often carried $30,000 in cash every day. How many trains were robbed?
   A) 10   B) 7   C) Zero
A. C) Zero.

Q. When did the first automobile reach the Grand Canyon?
A. In 1902 Oliver Lippincott thought it would take only a few hours to drive from Flagstaff to the South Rim on the old stagecoach road. It took him five days, lots of breakdowns, running out of gas and food, and being rescued by a team of horses. The good news is that he didn't have any problem finding a parking place.

...the same newspaper for which poet Walt Whitman once wrote.

Q. In 1919, when the Grand Canyon became a national park, how many tourists visited the park?
  A) 504,000   B) 104,000   C) 44,000
A. C) 44,000.

Q. What was the first year that visitation at the Grand Canyon exceeded one million people?
  A) 1956   B) 1965   C) 1980
A. A) 1956. By the 1990s visitation was reaching the five million mark.

Q. How did Phantom Ranch get its name?
A. It was named for Phantom Creek, which flows into Bright Angel Creek just upstream from Phantom Ranch. But how did Phantom Creek get its name? Some say it's because of the ghostly mist sometimes seen over the creek. Some say it's because the canyon that holds Phantom Creek is so narrow that you can walk right past it without noticing it. Some say there are ghosts there. Mary Colter, who built and named Phantom Ranch, said the phantom is a human-looking spire that towers 100 feet (30 m) over Phantom Creek.

Q. There's Hermits Rest, the Hermit Trail, Hermit Rapid, and the Hermit Shale. Who was the hermit?
A. A French-Canadian prospector named Louis Boucher. He was actually a friendly man who enjoyed showing tourists the canyon he loved. He took riders down his trail and had a tourist camp at a spring called Dripping Spring. Louis Boucher actually got two rapids and two trails named for him, since there is also a Boucher Rapid and a Boucher Trail. Architect Mary Colter designed Hermits Rest as a rest station for people riding mules up and down the Hermit Trail to the tourist camp built by the Santa Fe Railway.

Q. Grand Canyon National Park is the only national park to have its own public school that goes from 1st grade through high school. Other national parks are close enough to outside communities that the children of rangers and employees can be bused to schools, but the Grand Canyon is too isolated. A graduating high school class may have 15 to 20

Committed to realism, Mary Colter made Hopi House doorways short...

students. What is the name of the school's sports teams?
  A) The Phantoms   B) The Hermits   C) The Prospectors
A. A) The Phantoms.

Q. Beale Point was named for Edward Beale, an army officer who in the 1850s tried out a non-American animal for transportation in the American desert. What animal was it?
  A) Elephants   B) Zebras   C) Camels
A. C) Camels.

Q. True or false: The Grand Canyon holds a vast cave system full of Egyptian treasures, mummies, and hieroglyphics.
A. False. In 1909 a Phoenix newspaper published an April Fool's Day story about a Smithsonian expedition that had discovered a cave full of Egyptian artifacts in the Grand Canyon. Readers laughed, and the story was soon forgotten. Today the joke is on the occult books and websites that have resurrected this story as if it were real and continue adding new twists to it, including the claim that the National Park Service is covering up the truth.

Q. True or false: In World War II, U. S. dive bombers used El Tovar Hotel as a pretend target for training pilots. Dive-bombers swooped over the hotel and into the canyon.
A. True.

Q. Has an airplane ever landed inside the Grand Canyon?
A. Yes. In 1919, when airplanes were still a novelty and barnstormers were wowing crowds with stunt flying, a pilot named Royal Thomas flew his biplane into the canyon and landed near Plateau Point. A crude runway had been cleared for him, but it was a bumpy landing. He even managed to take off.

Q. Has anyone ever parachuted into the Grand Canyon?
A. Yes. In 1944 three airmen bailed out of a sputtering B-24 bomber and parachuted into a remote area inside the canyon. It took days and a difficult hike to rescue them. In 1993 two men tried to base jump into the Little Colorado River Gorge. Their parachutes became tangled, and one man hit the rocks and died.

...lots of tourists bump their heads going through.

Q. Has anyone ever hang glided into the Grand Canyon?
A. It's illegal, it's dangerous, and it's a long, hard carry back up, but in 1972 two guys couldn't resist. They landed near Phantom Ranch and were quickly arrested by a ranger, who handcuffed them and marched them out of the canyon.

Q. In the 1920s and 1930s the Fred Harvey Company ran bus tours from the Grand Canyon into the Navajo lands to the east. The roads were terrible and the buses sometimes broke down. The buses didn't have radios to signal for help. How did they summon help from the Fred Harvey garage at the South Rim?
A) Navajos on horses   B) Homing pigeons   C) Smoke signals
A. B) Homing pigeons. Each bus carried a cage with six pigeons. It took six pigeons, because hawks would usually kill a few on the flight home. Sometimes when buses tried to ford the Little Colorado River they would bog down in the water and sand. The drivers rushed outside to the running boards, where the pigeon cages were carried, to save the pigeons from drowning.

Q. In the 1920s astronomer George Ritchey wanted to build the world's greatest astronomical observatory. He had already helped build the Mount Wilson Observatory in California, where astronomer Edwin Hubble discovered the expanding universe. Ritchey became obsessed with the idea of building his new observatory on the rim of the Grand Canyon. In 1928 Ritchey sent an astronomer to the canyon to test out the viewing conditions there. Who was this astronomer?
A. Edwin Hubble. This was shortly after Hubble had discovered the expanding universe. This discovery is why the Hubble Space Telescope would be named in his honor.

Q. Did Hubble think the Grand Canyon was a good place for an observatory?
A. No. At the Grand Canyon, Hubble carried a telescope in the trunk of his car and set it up on the canyon rim. He soon decided that the Grand Canyon was a terrible place for an observatory. Astronomers need calm air, but the warm updrafts out of the canyon were very turbulent and would blur the images of stars. The new observatory

ended up being built atop Mt. Palomar near San Diego. Meanwhile *The New York Times* published a drawing of the planned observatory on the rim of the Grand Canyon and dubbed it the desert watchtower." A few years later Mary Colter built "the Desert View Watchtower on the spot planned for the Grand Canyon observatory.

Six amazing women and what they did at the Grand Canyon:
1. Ada Bass: A Boston-trained musician, she vacationed in Arizona in 1893 and fell in love with Grand Canyon prospector Bill Bass. She became the first white woman to raise a family at the Grand Canyon.
2. Mary Colter: A genius architect, she designed six public buildings at the Grand Canyon, blending the natural landscape with Native American themes.
3. Polly Mead Patraw: A botanist, Patraw became Grand Canyon National Park's first female ranger-naturalist in 1930, and only the second in the National Park Service.
4. & 5. Elzada Clover and Lois Jotter: The first women to boat the length of the Grand Canyon, in 1938. Clover was a botanist at the University of Michigan and Jotter was her student.
6. Georgie White Clark. Developed the potential of rubber rafts for Grand Canyon river running.

Q. Has anyone ever been married inside the Grand Canyon?
A. Thousands of couples have married on the rims of the canyon. A few more adventuresome couples, usually on river trips, have arranged to get married in the canyon bottom, at a favorite waterfall, grotto, or slot canyon. No one has kept any statistics on whether Grand Canyon weddings work out better than church or courthouse weddings. But one couple, Francis and Helen Line, made an anniversary hike to Phantom Ranch every year for six decades.

Q. In 1906 a sheepherder was driving 800 sheep to Lees Ferry to cross the Colorado River. When the thirsty sheep caught the scent of water, they stampeded towards the river, but blocking their path was a sheer cliff. What happened next?
A. When the leading sheep reached the cliff they tried to stop, but the stampede pushed hundreds of sheep over the cliff to

...and more in the summer.

their deaths. Their bones remained there for years.

Q. Which famous politician once went hunting near the North Rim, got stuck in the mud, and had to get towed out by a ranger?

   A) Barry Goldwater   B) Teddy Roosevelt   C) Bill Clinton

A. A) Senator Barry Goldwater. Ever since, that mud hole has been called "Goldwater Gulch."

Q. Until 1987 scenic air tours could fly anywhere they wanted inside the Grand Canyon. This was a safety hazard, since aircraft could appear suddenly from the rim or from side canyons. In 1986 a plane and a helicopter collided in midair inside the canyon, killing 25 people. Low-flying aircraft were also a source of noise pollution for hikers, river runners, the Havasupai Indians, and wildlife. Which politician introduced legislation to regulate air tours inside the Grand Canyon and in all national parks?

   A) Al Gore   B) Bill Clinton   C) John McCain

A. C) Senator John McCain. McCain also introduced the Grand Canyon Protection Act, which was meant to minimize damage to the river corridor caused by the operations of Glen Canyon Dam.

Q. Which Arizona family opened the grocery store on the South Rim in 1910?

   A) The Goldwaters   B) The Babbitts   C) The Bashas

A. B) The Babbitts. The Babbitt family was to northern Arizona what the Goldwater family was to southern Arizona, the leading mercantile family. The Babbitts ran trading posts on Indian lands, and they established the leading department store in Flagstaff, just as the Goldwaters owned the leading department store in Phoenix. Both families sent sons into politics. Bruce Babbitt became governor of Arizona and served as Secretary of the Interior in the Clinton administration from 1993 to 2001.

Q. Lees Ferry was named for John D. Lee, a Mormon pioneer who became a fugitive from federal law officers because of his role in the Mountain Meadows massacre. Mormon authorities sent John D. Lee to establish Lees Ferry in 1871 because it was so remote that no one would find him there, but a few years later he was captured and executed. A century later, two of his great-grandsons became very successful in national politics.

Though rustic looking, Desert View Watchtower...

Who were they?
A. Stewart Udall, who served as Secretary of the Interior in the Kennedy and Johnson administrations, and his brother Morris Udall, a longtime Arizona congressman and a candidate for the Democratic presidential nomination in 1976.

Q. Perhaps a million paintings have been done of the Grand Canyon. Which Grand Canyon painting is the most famous?
A. Actually, it was a painting that made the Grand Canyon famous. In the 1870s, when very few Americans had ever seen the Grand Canyon, the U.S. Congress paid artist Thomas Moran $10,000 to do a painting of the Grand Canyon. The painting was named "The Chasm of the Colorado" and was more than 7 feet (2.1 cm) tall and 12 feet (3.6 m) long. This painting was hung in the U. S. Capitol building, alongside Moran's giant painting of Yellowstone. For 30 years far more people saw Moran's Grand Canyon painting than saw the canyon itself.

Q. In his many paintings of the Grand Canyon, Thomas Moran took some "artistic license" with the canyon. What did he alter?
  A) He left out the geological strata
  B) He rearranged inner canyon features
  C) He colored everything golden-yellow
  D) All of the above
A. D) All of the above. Moran was trying to please an audience that was accustomed to European romantic paintings of green English countryside or the Alps. Few art lovers had ever seen the American Southwest, whose beauty is quite different. Moran used the same golden-yellow color scheme that J. M. W. Turner had used to paint the Italian countryside. After 1901, when the railroad allowed millions to see the Grand Canyon for themselves, Moran began painting the canyon more realistically.

Q. For many years, hikers on the North Kaibab Trail were astonished to find a kid's lemonade stand beside the trail, miles below the rim. What was it doing there?
A. It was at the home of Bruce Aiken, who ran the Roaring Springs pump house that supplies water to the rims. Bruce was a Greenwich Village-born artist who lived at Roaring Springs for

---

... is supported by a steel frame.

more than 30 years, where he and his wife Mary raised three children. Bruce's kids set up the lemonade stand, which hikers loved. Bruce became famous for his Grand Canyon paintings, which he often carried out of the canyon on his back.

Q. The Grand Canyon is one of the most photographed spots on Earth. Who took the first photograph of the Grand Canyon?
A. Timothy O'Sullivan, who learned photography under Civil War photographer Matthew Brady. O'Sullivan accompanied the 1871 Wheeler expedition to the Southwest. Sadly, most of O'Sullivan's Grand Canyon photos have been lost. It was John Hillers, who accompanied John Wesley Powell's second Colorado River expedition in 1872, who made the first extensive photographic study of the Grand Canyon. His photos have been used by modern scientists to make valuable then-and-now studies of changes in Grand Canyon rapids, beaches, and vegetation.

Q. What famous song was inspired by its writer's experiences at the Grand Canyon?
   A) "This Land is Your Land"
   B) "King of the Road"
   C) "Like a Rolling Stone"
A. B) "King of the Road." In 1953, at age 17, Roger Miller worked "pushin' broom" and picking up "old stogies" at Verkamp's gift shop on the canyon rim. He lived in a tiny "trailer for rent" beside the railroad tracks. A dozen years later, after Roger Miller was a big star, he returned to Verkamp's and told Jack and Betty Verkamp that "King of the Road" was inspired by his time at the Grand Canyon, when he was a "man of means, by no means."

As a curiosity Verkamp's store kept a meteorite on its front porch. One night pranksters scooted the meteorite against the front door, preventing Mr. Verkamp, who lived upstairs, from getting out. Another time, drunken cowboys stole it. But the meteorite was heavy iron, so it wasn't easy to lift. One night someone tried to steal it but must have dropped it on a hand because there was blood under the meteorite. Mr. Verkamp finally put a chain through the meteorite.

In the movie Grand Canyon, *Danny Glover talks about looking into the canyon...*

Q. Has any famous music been written about the Grand Canyon?
A. The most famous is American composer Ferde Grofe's 1931 "Grand Canyon Suite," a jazz-style classical work that brings out the clip-clopping of the mules on the trail. In the 1980s saxophonist Paul Winter was inspired by a Grand Canyon river trip to write the jazz-style suite "Canyon."

Q. The most popular novel about the Grand Canyon is Marguerite Henry's *Brighty of the Grand Canyon*. Was there really a Brighty?
A. Marguerite Henry's Brighty was based on a real burro that was abandoned by prospectors at the bottom of the canyon around 1890. This Brighty lived in the canyon and on the North Rim for another 30 years. He became very popular with canyon residents. Today there's a life-size bronze statue of Brighty inside Grand Canyon Lodge on the North Rim. It was donated by the movie company that filmed *Brighty of the Grand Canyon*. So many people have patted Brighty's nose that it's been polished shiny.

Q. In the 1960s a young writer worked as a ranger at Lees Ferry and as a fire lookout on the North Rim. He spent much of his time in the fire tower working on his writing. His most popular books, *Desert Solitaire* and *The Monkey Wrench Gang*, both involve the Grand Canyon. Who was he?
A. Edward Abbey. In both his fiction and nature writing, Abbey wrote about the beauties of Southwestern landscapes and about the need to protect the land from reckless development.

Q. Have any TV shows been shot at the Grand Canyon?
A. In 1959 Lassie came to the rescue at the Grand Canyon. There were actually five Lassies, who got their own room at the Bright Angel Lodge. In 1969 Lucille Ball ran Grand Canyon rapids in "Here's Lucy." In the 1970s it was "Grand Canyon or Bust" for the Brady Bunch.

Q. What was the first Hollywood movie filmed at the Grand Canyon?
A. In 1927, when both movies and running the Colorado River were fairly new, the Pathe-Bray Film Company went down the Colorado River to film a movie. It would be a

---

...Before filming, Glover hiked to Phantom Ranch so his lines would be real.

romantic melodrama called *The Bride of the Colorado River*. Foolishly, they ran the river in December and nearly froze and drowned. The movie was never finished.

Q. John Wayne's Hollywood debut film included a shot of him climbing out of the Grand Canyon, or at least a painting of it. What was the film?
A. *The Big Trail* in 1931.

Q. In 1960 Walt Disney filmed *Ten Who Dared* about the Powell expedition. In typical Disney style they added a character that wasn't on the real expedition. Who—or what—was it?
A. A cute little dog.

Q. What movie starring a young Brooke Shields was about finding gold in the Grand Canyon?
A. *Wanda Nevada*, which also starred Peter Fonda and featured a cameo appearance by his father, Henry Fonda, as a strange old prospector.

Q. Have movies pretended to be in the Grand Canyon?
A. Yes. Part of *Superman 3* was actually filmed a few miles up the Colorado River from the Grand Canyon. *Thelma and Louise* led viewers to believe that Thelma and Louise were hurtling their car into the Grand Canyon, when in fact the movie was filmed in Utah. This point was lost on several people whom Thelma and Louise inspired to commit suicide by driving cars into the Grand Canyon. Which brings us to our next chapter...

Thomas Moran painted the Grand Canyon hundreds of times. Georgia O'Keeffe, famous for Southwest art, never painted the Grand Canyon.

DEATH IN THE GRAND CANYON

Q. What's the most common form of death at the Grand Canyon?
A. In their study of deaths inside the canyon, *Over the Edge*, Dr. Thomas Myers and river guide Michael Ghiglieri found that aircraft accidents accounted for about 40 percent of fatalities. Accidental falls accounted for 16 percent of deaths, and boating and swimming deaths were 13 percent. Suicides were about 10 percent, and heat-related deaths on trails were about 10 percent.

Q. Who is most likely to die at the Grand Canyon?
    A) Children   B) The elderly   C) Young males
A. C) Young males, by a huge margin. Dozens of young males have fallen to their death at the Grand Canyon but only one child. River fatalities are 90 percent male and about 40 percent under the age of 28. Frequently the victims are trying to show off, or acting with foolish disregard for safety.

Q. How many people accidentally fall off the rim every year?
A. From one to five people.

> Bad joke: How often do people fall into the Grand Canyon?
> Answer: Only once.

Q. Which is deadlier: climbing Mt. Everest or hiking and river running in the Grand Canyon?
A. About 190 people have died climbing Mt. Everest as of 2008, but more than 200 have died hiking and river running in the Grand Canyon.

Q. What's the deadliest mile on the Colorado River?
A) Crystal Rapid   B) Lava Falls   C) The riffles near Phantom Ranch

---

Several victims of Grand Canyon flash floods have been veteran hikers.

A. C) It's only one mile between Phantom Ranch and the base of the Bright Angel Trail, but in the summer heat some hikers try to swim this mile so they don't have to hike or they just try to cool off in the river here. A dozen people have drowned in this stretch. That's twice as many deaths as in the Grand Canyon's deadliest rapid, Crystal. It's not the riffles that kill, it's the river's coldness and powerful currents, which soon induce hypothermia and overpower even the strongest swimmers.

Q. What's the total number of people who have drowned in the Grand Canyon?

 A) 26   B) 56   C) 94

A. C) 94, as of 2013. And 83 of these, or 90%, were males.

Q. Of the 94 drownings in the Grand Canyon, what percent were not wearing life jackets?

 A) 50 percent B) 60 percent   C) 75 percent

A. C) About 75 percent were not wearing life jackets.

Q. In 1983 the Bureau of Reclamation failed to anticipate the amount of water entering Lake Powell and had to release an emergency flood of 93,000 cfs down the Colorado River. This flood turned Crystal Rapid into a monster that could flip a 33-foot-long (10 m), 4-ton motorized raft. In a period of a few days, how many of these rafts were flipped in Crystal Rapid?

 A) 1   B) 3   C) 4

A. C) Four of the giant rafts were flipped in a few days, throwing 90 people into the water, injuring 15, and killing one. In the entire history of Grand Canyon river running, about 25 of these giant rafts have flipped.

Q. How high was the wave in Crystal Rapid that flipped these rafts?

 A) 15 feet (4.5 m) B) 20 feet (6 m) C) 25 feet (7.6 m)

A. C) 25 feet (7.6 m) feet high, and 60 feet (18 m) wide. This was no ordinary wave but a hole where water recirculates and can stop boats dead.

Q. Seven people have drowned after accidentally falling into the river from river camps, usually at night. What was the main

---

Grand Canyon's first ranger-naturalist, Glen Sturdevant...

factor leading to their death?
   A) Darkness   B) Alcohol   C) Tripping on rocks
A. B) Alcohol. Almost all victims were seriously intoxicated.
Many fatal falls from the rim also involved alcohol.

Q. How did a flower drown someone in the Grand Canyon?
A. Datura is a beautiful, large, white desert flower. Native
Americans use it in vision quests, but they also use centuries
of caution and expertise because datura is a potent neuro-
toxin that can induce blindness, seizures, and death. Even
Native Americans have died from it. Datura is also known as
"locoweed" for its effect on horses. In 1971 some hippies camping at Phantom Ranch swallowed some datura. One person had
wild hallucinations, seemed to think he could walk on the Colorado River, and drowned.

Q. What was the worst aircraft accident at the Grand Canyon?
A. In 1956, before commercial air routes were as well regu-
lated as today, two passenger airliners collided over the Grand
Canyon and crashed into the canyon near the mouth of the
Little Colorado River. All 128 people on board died. This was the
worst airline accident in American history up to that time. Removing the bodies required helicopters and mountain climbers.
For years you could see wreckage gleaming in the sun. Today
many small pieces of debris remain scattered over the cliffs.

Q. Two private pilots have crashed planes inside the Grand
Canyon for the same unlikely cause. What was the cause?
A) Hit by lightning   B) Ran out of gas   C) Collided with condors
A. B) They ran out of gas. In 1978 the first of these pilots
crashed inside the canyon, killing all three people aboard. Two
years later the other pilot got luckier and survived.

Q. In 1982 a helicopter pilot failed to notice the tram cable at
Lees Ferry and hit it, plunging into the Colorado River, killing
three people. Three years later, and only 4 miles downstream, a
helicopter hit Navajo Bridge, killing two. Both helicopters were
attempting the same thing. What was it?
   A) Stunt flying   B) Filming movies   C) Police chases
A. B) Filming movies.

...drowned in a river accident.

Q. Which is deadlier at the Grand Canyon: lightning or cameras?
A. Cameras. Several people have died while posing for photos right on the rim. A few lost their balance. Others continued stepping backward until they stepped right over the edge. Only two people have been killed by lightning, though more have been struck.

Q. Robert Spangler's wife, Sharon Spangler, wrote a book about hiking in the Grand Canyon. After their divorce, Robert married a woman named Donna, and later he murdered her in the Grand Canyon. What was his murder weapon?
A. He pushed her off a trail and over a 160-foot (48 m) cliff. Only when Robert Spangler was dying of cancer did he confess.

Q. How many people commit suicide at the Grand Canyon every year?
A. One or two on average, but some years see four or five. Usually it's by jumping off the rim. But one person jumped out of a sightseeing helicopter.

Q. What percent of canyon suicides occur by people driving cars off the rim of the Grand Canyon?
   A) 5   B) 10   C) 20
A. C) About 20 percent. In the year after the movie *Thelma and Louise* came out on video, there were three car suicides. Cars have plunged as far as 1,500 feet (457 m) into the canyon.

Q. In the first two cases of people committing suicide by driving off the rim (in 1967 and 1974) their cars had one thing in common. What was it?
A) Both were rental cars B) Both were Corvettes C) Both were stolen
A. A) Both were rental cars from Hertz. In one of those cases, a couple drove their favorite motorcycle to the canyon and then rented the car. It seems they couldn't bear to wreck their motorcycle.

In 1983 a professional boxer dove over Havasu Waterfall...

Q. Of people who committed suicide at the canyon, what percent have been wanted for crimes?

    A) 7 percent   B) 17 percent   C) 47 percent

A. B) 17 percent

Q. Which place has seen more suicides: the Grand Canyon, Niagra Falls, or the Golden Gate Bridge?

A. The Golden Gate Bridge has seen more than 1,300 suicides, Niagara Falls has seen more than 400, and the Grand Canyon has seen 75, as of 2013. A survey done between 2003 and 2009 showed that the Grand Canyon had more suicides than any other national park, but this was only 11 out of a national total of 194.

Q. In 2009, the deadliest year for hiking deaths in the canyon, ten people died. How many of them drowned while trying to swim across the Colorado River?

A. Three of them, all young men, trying to swim the river at Phantom Ranch.

In 1966 a ten-year-old bicyclist was riding on Hermit Road, which sometimes runs very close to the canyon edge. He was going too fast and missed a curve and flew right off the rim. He fell 120 feet and landed on a talus slope. Amazingly, while he was seriously injured, he survived.

Legendary boatman Bert Loper died of a heart attack while rowing the Grand Canyon.

Grand Canyon historian Scott Thybony suggests that author Ambrose Bierce, who vanished in 1914, actually committed suicide in the Grand Canyon.

...he landed on his back, and died.